Medical Law in Norway

Medical Law in Norway

Karl Harald Søvig

This book was originally published as a monograph in the International Encyclopaedia of Laws/Medical Law.

Founding Editor: Roger Blanpain
General Editor: Frank Hendrickx
Volume Editor: Herman Nys; Associate Editor: Tom Goffin

Wolters Kluwer

Published by:
Kluwer Law International B.V.
PO Box 316
2400 AH Alphen aan den Rijn
The Netherlands
E-mail: lrs-sales@wolterskluwer.com
Website: www.wolterskluwer.com/en/solutions/kluwerlawinternational

Sold and distributed by:
Wolters Kluwer Legal & Regulatory U.S.
7201 McKinney Circle
Frederick, MD 21704
United States of America
E-mail: customer.service@wolterskluwer.com

ISBN 978-94-035-1576-2

e-Book: ISBN 978-94-035-1276-1
web-PDF: ISBN 978-94-035-1286-0

The Author

Prof. Dr juris Karl Harald Søvig graduated from the Faculty of Law, University of Bergen (cand. jur. 1995; Dr juris 2005). He has been working at the Faculty of Law, University of Bergen since 1996, and since 2009 as a professor. He is currently the Dean of the Faculty. He has previously worked as a temporary judge at the district and high court and as ad hoc chairman of the county board. He wrote his dissertation on detention of alcoholics and drug addicts, *Incarceration of Alcohol or Drug Addicts: The Norwegian Social Services Act Sections 6-2 till 6-3*. His research has focused on different forms of coercive measures within the welfare state, as well as rights of the children, and provision of health services to irregular migrants. Søvig is a former guest professor at Changchun University of Science and Technology (Changchun, China) and chair of the European Association of Health Law (EAHL).

The Author

Table of Contents

List of Abbreviations

ECHR	European Convention on Human Rights
ECtHR	European Court of Human Rights
EEA	European Economic Area
EFTA	European Free Trade Association
EU	European Union
HLY	Healthy Life Years
HPA	Health Personnel Act
MNMA	Members of the Norwegian Medical Association
NAFKAM	National Research Centre in Complementary and Alternative Medicine
NATO	North Atlantic Treaty Organization
NOU	Norges Offentlige Utredninger (Official Norwegian Reports)
Ot.prp.	Odelstingsproposisjon (legislative bill sent by the government to the Odelsting (chamber of the Storting) for consideration, until 2009)
PRA	Patients' Rights Act
Prop. L	Proposisjon til Stortinget – Lovvedtak (legislative bill sent by the government to the Storting for consideration, from 2009)
UN	United Nations

Abbreviations and Index over Norwegian Acts (*see* paragraph 27 for Sources of Translations of Legislation into English)

Short Title	*Translated Full Title*
Abortion Act	Act relating to Termination of Pregnancy (13 June 1975 No. 50)
Alternative Treatment Act	Act relating to the Alternative Treatment of Disease, Illness, etc. (27 June 2003 No. 64)

List of Abbreviations

Autopsy Act	Act relating to Autopsy and Release of Bodies to Education and Research (7 May 2015 No. 26)
Biobank Act	Act relating to Biobanks (21 February 2003 No. 12)
Census Act	Act relating to Directory of Residents (9 December 2016 No. 88)
Child Welfare Act	Act relating to Child Welfare Services (17 July 1992 No. 100)
Children Act	Act relating to Children and Parents (8 April 1981 No. 7)
Civil Procedure Code	Act relating to Mediation and Procedure in Civil Disputes (17 June 2005 No. 90)
Compensation Act	Act relating to Compensation (13 June 1969 No. 26)
Communicable Diseases Act	Act relating to Control of Communicable Diseases (5 August 1994 No. 55)
Control of Marketing and Contract Terms Act	Act relating to the Control of Marketing and Contract Terms and Conditions, etc. (9 January 2009 No. 2)
Criminal Procedure Code	Act relating to Legal Procedure in Criminal Cases (22 May 1981 No. 25)
Dental Care Act	Act relating to Dental Health Services (3 June 1984 No. 54)
Education Act	Act relating to Primary and Secondary Education (17 July 1998 No. 61)
Ethics Research Act	Act relating to Ethics in Research (24 April 2017 No. 23)
Equality and Anti-Discrimination Act	Act relating to Equality and a Prohibition against Discrimination (16 June 2017 No. 51)
Freedom of Information Act	Act relating to the Right of Access to Documents held by Public Authorities and Public Undertakings (19 May 2006 No. 15)
Guardianship Act	Act relating to Guardianship (26 March 2010 No. 9)
Gender Change Act	Act relating to Change of Legal Gender (17 June 2016 No. 46)
Health and Care Services Act	Act relating to Municipal Health and Care Services, etc. (24 June 2011 No. 30)
Health Authorities and Health Trust Act	Act relating to Health Authorities and Health Trusts (15 June 2001 No. 93)
Health Personnel Act (HPA)	Act relating to Health Personnel, etc. (2 July 1999 No. 64)

Health Register Act	Act relating to Personal Health Data Filing Systems and the Processing of Personal Health Data (20 June 2014 No. 43)
Health Research Act	Act relating to Medical and Health Research (20 June 2008 No. 44)
Health Supervision Act	Act relating to Public supervision of Health and Care Services, etc. (15 December 2017 No. 107)
Human Rights Act	Act relating to the Strengthening of the Status of Human Rights in Norwegian Law (21 May 1999 No. 30)
Insurance Contracts Act	Act relating to Insurance Contracts (16 June 1989 No. 69)
Legal Aid Act	Act relating to Free Legal Aid (13 June 1980 No. 35)
Medical Equipment Act	Act relating to Medical Equipment (12 January 1995 No. 6)
Medicines Act	Act relating to Medicines, etc. (4 December 1992 No. 132)
Mental Health Care Act (MHA)	Act relating to the Provision and Implementation of Mental Health Care (2 July 1999 No. 62)
National Insurance Act	Act relating to National Insurance (28 February 1997 No. 19)
Parliamentary Ombudsperson Act	Act relating to the Parliamentary Ombudsperson for Public Administration (18 June 2021 No. 121)
Patients' Injury Act	Act relating to Compensation in Cases of Patients' Injury (15 June 2001 No. 53)
Patients' Rights Act (PRA)	Act relating to Patients' and Users' Rights (2 July 1999 No. 63)
Penal Code	The Penal Code (20 May 2005 No. 28)
Personal Data Act	Act relating to Personal Data (15 June 2018 No. 38)
Pharmacy Act	Act relating to Pharmacies (2 June 2000 No. 39)
Public Administration Act (PAA)	Act relating to Procedure in Cases concerning the Public Administration (10 February 1967)
Public Health Act	Act relating to Public Health Efforts (24 June 2011 No. 29)
Road Traffic Act	Act relating to Road Traffic (18 June 1965 No. 4)
Specialized Health Care Act	Act relating to Specialized Health Services, etc. (2 July 1999 No. 61)
Sterilisation Act	Act relating to Sterilisation (3 June 1977 No. 57)
Transplantation Act	Act relating to Donation and Transplantation of Organs, Cells and Tissues (7 May 2015 No. 25)

List of Abbreviations

Working Environment Act	Act relating to Working Environment, Working Hours and Employment Protection, etc. (17 June 2005 No. 62)

General Introduction

§1. General Background of the Country

I. Geography

1. Norway is situated north in Europe on the western part of the Scandinavian Peninsula. The mainland of Norway is surrounded by the coast on the west side and shares borders with Russia, Finland and Sweden on the east part. In addition to the mainland comes the island Jan Mayen and the island group of Spitsbergen, both situated north and west of Norway in the Artic area. Spitsbergen is regulated by the Svalbard treaty that gives Norway full sovereignty, but parties entering into the treaty certainly have several rights based on non-discrimination.[1] In addition to the above-mentioned areas considered as the 'realm' of Norway pursuant to the Constitution comes Bouvet Island, Peter I Island and Queen Maud Land in the Antarctic. They are deemed to be Norwegian dependencies.

2. Norway has a very elongated shape, with a long and rugged coastline. The mainland covers 13° latitude, from 58°N to more than 71°N (Svalbard north to 81°N). Large areas are dominated by the Scandinavian Mountains; the average elevation is 460 m and 32% of the mainland is located above the treeline. From western Norway and to the north the fjords are a central element of the coastline, with Sognefjorden as the most well-known. It stretches 205 km inland from the ocean. Although situated in Northern Europe, the climate is warmer than the latitude should indicate due to the Gulf Stream. Historically, fish and forests were the most important natural resources. They are still important, and the fish industry has developed to also include sea farms. Hydroelectric power came during the industrialization and oil and natural gas were discovered in the late 1960s. The petroleum industry accounts for around a quarter of Norway's gross domestic product.

3. Norway is a middle-sized country (ranked as No. 61 of the world's countries by area) with a small population (ranked as No. 117), cf. paragraph 16 *infra*.[2] Large parts of Norway are scarcely populated, which can be of challenge in cases of emergency healthcare. The transport distances may be long, and weather conditions can

1. *See* Geir Ulfstein, *The Svalbard Treaty: From Terra Nullius to Norwegian Sovereignty* (Scandinavian University Press 1995).
2. https://en.wikipedia.org/wiki/List_of_countries_and_dependencies_by_area# (Svalbard and Spitsbergen are excluded) and https://en.wikipedia.org/wiki/List_of_countries_and_dependencies_by_population (both last retrieved 10 Jul 2022).

prevent transport. An ongoing political discussion in Norway relates to the functions of smaller hospitals, especially regarding eligible surgery. Concentration in larger units is seen as necessary to provide sufficient critical mass of patients in order to secure quality, while critics claim that this can lead to more severe health conditions while patients are in transport and deprive citizens in rural areas of basic health services.

II. Cultural Composition

4. The Scandinavian countries are rather homogeneous societies. Despite some differences between the three countries, both due to history and recent developments – e.g., the immigration rate has been much higher in Sweden than in Denmark and Norway – the referral to 'Scandinavian culture' is rather common. The term 'Nordic' is also used, including Iceland and Finland. The Nordic countries also have an institutional cooperation through the Nordic Council (*see* paragraph 15 *infra*).

5. The Scandinavian countries have a common history and being in different forms of unions since the Viking ages. The languages in the three countries form a dialectic continuum, where one can understand each other languages, although English, to some extent has taken over as a Scandinavian cross-border language for younger generations. The vast majority of the Scandinavian population descended from the North Germanic tribes, and many words in the Scandinavian language have a German origin.

6. However, the Scandinavian Peninsula was inhabited prior to the immigration from the south. The Sami population is an indigenous Finno-Ugric people inhabiting the Arctic area of Sápmi, which today encompasses parts of far northern Norway, Sweden, Finland, the Kola Peninsula of Russia, and the border area between south and middle Sweden and Norway. The Sami are the only indigenous people of Scandinavia recognized and protected under the international conventions of indigenous peoples. The total Sami population is estimated to be 50,000–80,000, whereas 40,000 are living in Norway.

7. Of the just above 5.4 million population in Norway (*see* paragraph 16), the immigrants amount to 18.9%. At the beginning of 2022, there were 819,356 immigrants and 205,819 Norwegian-born to immigrant parents in Norway.[3] Of the total of 1,025,175 immigrants 41% are coming from EU27/EEA, Great Britain, USA, Canada, Australia and New Zealand, while 59% are coming from other parts of the world. Persons with an immigrant background from Poland make up the largest group in Norway with nearly 120,000.

3. Figures from Statistics Norway, https://www.ssb.no/innvbef (last retrieved 10 Jul 2022).

III. Political System

8. Norway is a constitutional monarchy. The sagas relate to how King Harald Hårfagre (Harald Fairhair) (c. AD 865–933) united Norway as a kingdom. After a stable period in the second half of the eleventh century, the Norwegian realm was haunted by civil wars from 1130 till 1223. After this, a united and storing Norwegian state emerged. As regards legislation, the codification of the law was still by provinces (the Gulating Compilation of Law, etc.) until King Magnus Lagabøte's (Magnus the Lawmender's) Code of the Realm of 1274 and Code of the Cities of 1276. Norway was in a union with Denmark from 1380 until 1814. Absolute monarchy was introduced in 1661 and enacted in the Royal Law of 1665. In Norwegian constitutional law theory, the traditional view is that Norway was an independent kingdom during the whole period of the union, even though Denmark was the stronger party in practice. Denmark-Norway was on the losing side in the Napoleonic Wars, and the cession of Norway to Sweden was one of the conditions stipulated in the Treaty of Kiel of January 1814. The failure to involve the Norwegian people in this process resulted in opposition in Norway. Prince Christian Frederik, who was the Danish-Norwegian king's governor in Norway, summoned representatives of the elite of Norwegian society to a meeting at Eidsvoll on 16 February 1814 (the Meeting of Notables). The participants at the meeting agreed to reject the peace treaty and to convene a constituent assembly with broad representation (the Constituent Assembly). The Constituent Assembly adopted the Norwegian Constitution on 16 May 1814. The next day, Christian Frederik was elected King of Norway and was presented with a signed copy of the Constitution. That is why Norway celebrates its National Day on 17 May.

9. Sweden regarded Norway's independence as a breach of the Treaty of Kiel, and, following a short war, the Convention of Moss was signed in August 1814. The Convention was based on the Eidsvoll Constitution being retained, but with such amendments as were necessary to adapt it to the union with Sweden that Norway was required to enter into. The Norwegian parliament, the Storting, adopted the amendments to the constitution on 4 November 1814.

10. The union with Sweden was characterized by conflict between the Storting and the Swedish Crown. Several distinctive features of the Constitution can be traced back to this power struggle. In the end, it was a disagreement about the management of foreign affairs that led to its dissolution. From 7 June 1905, Norway was again an independent country. The Constitution from 1814 had been a core legal document throughout the union, and the reluctance to change the constitution was to some extent kept afterwards. The inflexibility of the wording in many areas called for an innovative interpretation. However, in recent years important principles established by customs have been codified. Additionally, a major reform was made in 2014 as part of the bicentennial. The human right's protection was strengthened and the language was updated from old-fashioned Norwegian (with similarities to

Danish) to modern Norwegian. The Constitution is now articulated in both versions of the written Norwegian language, which are equally authentic.[4]

11. The Storting has 169 seats, and general elections are held every fourth year.[5] The parliament has three main tasks: to adopt general norms through legislation, to regulate the State's finances through appropriations and taxation, and to control and supervise the executive branch of government. Until 2009 legislation passed the Storting under a form of bi-cameral system (the chambers were composed according to the same election), but this was replaced by a procedure of two readings by plenary sessions of the parliament. Every act must be ratified by the government (King) to become valid. Such sanction is normally given without any second review of the act.

12. Historically, the executed power was vested with the King in person, who was surrounded by his advisers. Gradually, the personal power declined, and today the government decides in all matters of political interests.[6] However, the decisions are made in the name of the King and his signature is a condition for a valid decision. The Government is formed by the party/parties that have a majority of the seats in the Storting or constitute a minority capable of governing. Thus the Government is indirectly selected by the electorate. A general election can lead to a change of government, but not necessarily. Additionally, there can be a change of government other than in connection with a general election if a situation should arise where the Government no longer has the confidence of the Storting. Between the World Wars, minority governments were common, with frequent shifts. After the Second World War, majority government – with the labour party as sole companion – was dominant until the mid-1960s, followed by a period of minority governments. The last governments (from 2005) have been majority coalitions.

13. Norway has three levels of administration. The executive power is vested with the King and today conducted by the government, headed by the Prime Minister. The ministers are the head of their ministry (some ministries are divided between ministers). Several administrative bodies are organized as subordinate agencies (like the Norwegian Directorate of Health), while others are partly impartial (*see* examples in paragraphs 150 and 264 *infra*). Turning to the regional level, Norway is divided into nineteen counties, which are separate entities. Historically, the counties have been responsible for large parts of health services, including the hospitals. After a major reform in 2001 the responsibility of hospitals was transferred to the state level (*see* paragraph 43 *infra*), but the counties are currently still responsible for dental health. There are from 1 January 2020, 356 municipalities in Norway, and an ongoing – and debated – reform has reduced the number from 428

4. *See* Karen Gammelgaard & Eirik Holmøyvik (eds), *Writing Democracy: The Norwegian Constitution 1814–2014* (Berghahn 2014).
5. For a presentation of the parliament in English, *see* https://www.stortinget.no/en/In-English (accessed 10 Jul 2022).
6. For a presentation of the government in English, *see* https://www.regjeringen.no/en/id4/ (accessed 10 Jul 2022).

municipalities in 2016. The municipalities are responsible for different forms of services to the citizens, including primary healthcare. The reform has aimed at reducing the smallest municipalities, but there is still a wide variety in the populations of municipalities, differing from just above 200 citizens to about 700,000 (Oslo). Small municipalities will often have to enter into different forms of cooperation with their neighbours regarding provision of welfare services. The ongoing reform has also reduced the number of counties, and there are, from 1 January 2020, 11 counties, a reduction from 19 in 2016. As indicated, the reform is a political issue, and the current government is taking measures to reverse several of the mergers.

The counties and municipalities are autonomous entities headed by elected councils (elections every fourth year between the parliament elections). The counties and municipalities have self-government. After many years of dispute, a proclamation of local self-government was taken into the constitution (section 49, second paragraph) but the specific provisions regarding the local democratically elected level shall be laid down by ordinary legislation by the parliament. Taxation to a large extent takes place at the state level, and the counties and municipalities are dependent on state funding to carry out their legal obligation.

14. While Norway was neutral through the First World War, the attempt for a similar position failed when the country was invaded by Germany on 9 April 1940. The Germans occupied Norway throughout the war, and the occupation ended on 8 May 1945. The invasion and occupation illustrated the need for different forms of international instruments and institutions, especially for a small country like Norway. The United Nations (UN) has from its founding been an anchor for Norwegian foreign policy. Military, Norway entered the North Atlantic Treaty Organization (NATO) from its establishment (1949). NATO membership has been a cornerstone in Norwegian security policy. During the cold war, Norway also had a special position as a country-sharing border with the Soviet Union.

15. At the regional level, the Nordic Council was intended to play a major role.[7] It was formed after the Second World War to promote cooperation between the five Nordic countries. Its first concrete result was the introduction in 1952 of a common labour market and free movement across borders without passports for the countries' citizens. Further strengthening, especially regarding economic cooperation failed and Denmark and Norway applied for membership in the European Union (EU, *see infra*). However, the Council stills play a major role and it is a comprehensive regional partnership, despite the fact that it has no legislative power on its own. In addition to the five Nordic countries, the Faroe Islands, Greenland, and Åland work together in this cooperation. The Baltic States (Estonia, Latvia and Lithuania) are observers.

16. Norway was a founding member of the Council of Europe and the cooperation within the council is still important for Norway. Turning to the EU, Norway's relation has been a political controversial topic. In two referendums (1972 and

---

7. For a presentation of the Nordic Council in English, *see* http://www.norden.org/en/nordic-council (accessed 10 Jul 2022).

1994) the general public has turned down draft agreements of entering into the EU. Norway is a member of the European Free Trade Association (EFTA), together with Switzerland, Iceland and Luxembourg. Together with the two latter states, Norway has been part of the European Economic Area (EEA) Agreement from 1992 between these three EFTA States and the Member States of the EU.[8] New parties have entered into the EEA Agreement in pace with enlargements of the union, and several states have shifted side from the EFTA to the EU. The core content of the EEA Agreement is to give the parties access to the common market, with some exceptions (fish and agriculture). Additionally, Norway has entered into EU agreements on specific fields, like the Schengen regulations.[9] Norway is therefore to a large extent bound by EU legislation, although the Storting has kept its formal position as the legislator.

17. In 2019, the government announced that over the course of many years, the Norwegian Labour and Welfare Administration (NAV) has applied the requirement of stay in Norway under the Norwegian National Insurance Act for recipients of sickness benefit, attendance allowance and work assessment allowance in a manner contrary to the social security regulation (Regulation No. 883/2004) and other EEA law instruments. The case received massive attention in the media and in the political system. It led to investigations, and court cases, since many persons were convicted for benefit fraud.[10] It was in many ways an eye opener regarding the impact if EEA and shortcomings of the understanding of its impact, also among academic scholars.

IV. Population and Vital Statistics

18. Norway has a population of 5.4 million people (5,435,536 persons were registered as living in Norway as on 1 January 2022).[11] The net immigration is 19,650 persons (for 2020). The GDB per capita is NOK 765,836 (approx. EUR 75,000) and the consumer index is 6.3% (from June 2021 to June 2022). The unemployment rate

---

8. *See* Carl Baudenbacher (ed.), *The Handbook of EEA Law* (Springer 2015) and Finn Arnesen et al., *Agreement on the European Economic Area: A Commentary* (Nomos/Hart 2018).
9. For a review of the consequences of the EEA Agreement and Norway's other agreements with the EU, *see* the report from a governmental appointed expert committee, NOU 2012:2 *Innenfor og utenfor. Norges avtaler med EU (Outside and Inside. Norway's Agreements with the European Union).* The abstract is translated into English, *see* https://www.regjeringen.no/contentassets/5d3982d042a2472eb1b20639cd8b2341/en-gb/pdfs/nou201220120002000en_pdfs.pdf. For more information regarding Norway and EU, *see* the webpage of the mission of Norway to the EU, https://www.norway.no/en/eu#.Vl69AaPKyUk (both accessed 10 Jul 2022).
10. *See*, NOU 2020: 9 *Blindsonen: Gransking av feilpraktiseringen av folketrygdlovens oppholdskrav ved reiser i EØS-området* (Blindspot: Review of the misapplication of the national insurance act requirement of stay in Norway when travel in the EEA area) and NOU 2021: 8 *Trygd over landegrensene – Gjennomføring og synliggjøring av Norges trygdekoordineringsforpliktelser* (Cross-border social security – Implementation and visibility of Norway's obligation to coordinate social security systems), the first with a summary in English.
11. For a presentation of a selection of vital statistics in English, *see* the website of Statistics Norway https://www.ssb.no/en/ (accessed 10 Jul 2022).

is 3.2% (as on June 2022). Norway is rich in natural resources, especially fish and oil/gas. Export revenues from oil and gas are important factors of the economy (*see supra* paragraph 2).

19. The total area of mainland Norway is 385,170 km^2, while Spitsbergen is 61,022 km^2 and Jan Mayen is 377 km^2. The Norwegian coastal line is 100,915 km, being the second largest in the world (behind Canada). Besides the economic zone based on the mainland, Norway has established a Fisheries Protection Zone outside Spitsbergen and it also lays claim to the continental shelf. Both of these claims are disputed in the international law context. Outside Jan Mayen, Norway has established an economic zone (the borders between Greenland, belonging to Denmark, were settled by the International Court of Justice).

20. The life expectancy for men is 81 years and for women, 84 years (in 2018).[12] Healthy Life Years (HLY) is an established indicator of expected health and is calculated from data on mortality and sickness. The number of HLY has increased more than the life expectancy and the average is now over 70 years. The life expectancy is partly related to smoking habits, and there has been a significant decline since the 1970s. In 2019, 10% of the adult population were daily smokers, and 13% used snuff (a tobacco product common in Norway and Sweden). In the last twenty years, Norwegians have become heavier (figures from 2017). Overweight is a body mass index (BMI) between 25 and 30 kg/m^2. Obesity is a BMI of 30 kg/m^2 or above. In total, between 15% and 20% of children are overweight or obese (about 1 in 6 children).[13] There are signs that the trend has levelled out. In total, 1 in 4 young people (about 25%) are overweight or obese. There are indications that the proportion is increasing. Regional studies indicate that about 25% of men and 40% of women have normal weight. The majority of men and women are overweight or obese, and the proportion is greatest among men. About 25% of men and 21% of women aged 40–45 are obese.

While alcoholism was previously a major health problem, alcohol intake has declined in the last generation. This trend is now changing (figures from 2019). Since the early 1990s, the consumption of alcohol has increased by approximately 40%, mostly among women and the elderly.[14] Due to high taxation of alcohol, it is also a significant unregistered consumption from cross-border trade (Sweden) and duty-free sales at Norwegian airports. On average, Norwegians aged over 15 years drink about 8 l of pure alcohol per year (including estimated unregistered consumption). Still, the alcohol consumption in Norway (registered and estimates of unregistered) is lower than in most other European countries.

---

12. For information regarding health conditions, *see* https://www.ssb.no/en/helse (accessed 10 Jul 201 9).
13. Norwegian Institute of Public Health, Overweight and obesity in Norway, https://www.fhi.no/en/op/hin/lifestyle/overweight-and-obesity-in-norway---/#main-points (accessed 10 Jul 2022).
14. Norwegian Institute of Public Health, Alcohol and other psychoactive substances in Norway https://www.fhi.no/en/op/hin/lifestyle/alcohol-and-other-psychoactive-subs/#studies-of-alcohol-consumption (accessed 10 Jul 2022).

V. Social and Cultural Values

21. As mentioned earlier, the social and cultural values are rather similar in the Scandinavian – and Nordic – countries. The Viking era leaves the impression of a quite violent behaviour, but at least in modern times Norway has been a rather tranquil society, with modest crime rates. Norway was from medieval age a rather poor country, with difficult conditions for farming. As in many other European countries, the Black Death was a pandemic with a devastating impact. Estimates suggest that it bisected the Norwegian population. The combination of a poor country in union with Denmark – being stronger both politically and economically – has given the origin to phrases like the 400 years night in Norwegian history. However, situated in the outskirts of the continent, Norway was less involved in warfare than many other countries.

22. It is difficult to identify social and cultural values without being too superficial or stereotype. Additionally, the Norwegian society is less homogenous than previous just a generation ago. Immigration, as well as informal impact from other culture through travelling, media, etc. has led to greater diversity. Norway is still a rather equal society. The farmers have from medieval age to a large extent owned their land, and the feudal system was never introduced as in Central Europe. The Constitution abolished the nobility hierarchy. Voting rights provided to self-owning farmers from 1814 also indicate an egalitarian approach. General suffrage for men was introduced in 1898, for women in 1913. Even though not being in the forefront regarding voting rights for women, equal treatment of gender is a part of the country's contemporary values. The employment rate for women is among the highest in Europe.[15] This is partly due to legislative measures like modest affirmative action and lengthy maternity leaves, but it is the combination of different tools and a cultural climate that fertilizes this development. However, challenges remain. The committee supervising the Convention on the Elimination of All Forms of Discrimination against Women identified, *inter alia,* violence against women as one main area of concern.[16] Another indication of a rather equal society is the limited income differences, which are found in all Scandinavian countries.[17]

23. The distribution of public services is to a large extent universal, which also could be seen as a form of equal treatment. The welfare state has its origin in the protection of factory workers during the late parts of the industrial revolution, but the general development started after the Second World War. Although it has been several political controversies, all political parties have taken part in the built-up of the welfare state.[18] The Scandinavian welfare society has to some extent also been

15. *See* https://ec.europa.eu/eurostat/databrowser/view/LFSI_EMP_A__custom_3051620/default/table?lang=en (accessed 10 Jul. 2019).
16. *See* the committee's concluding observation to Norway, 22 Nov. 2019 (CEDAW/C/NOR/CO/9), and especially para. 39 for health issues.
17. *See* http://www.oecd.org/social/inequality.htm#income (accessed 10 Jul. 2022).
18. Nanna Kildal & Stein Kuhnle (eds), *Normative Foundations of the Welfare State The Nordic Experience* (Routledge 2005).

used as inspiration for other countries. As in other parts of the world a contemporary issue is the sustainability of the welfare state, where an ageing population and increased pension costs are two major trends. A particularity in Norway is the strong organization on both sides of the labour market. This has also led to a system where negations are first carried out for the export industries, in order to avoid a raise in salaries unbearable for the competition.

24. Norwegians can be regarded as rather nationalistic, and the celebration of the National Day (Constitution Day: 17 May) is a major national event. This nationalism may also be linked to a high degree in trust to different forms of public bodies. There is a confidence that the authorities should intervene if people are not capable of taking care of themselves. This kind of trust also goes to different forms or organizations and fellow citizens.

25. The reformation was introduced in Denmark and Norway in 1536. The church played, and continued to play, an important role in the development of the society. The Lutheran approach meant that the church partly was a body within the state, with the King also as head of the church. The role of the church has declined in many aspects. Additionally, immigration has led to diversity within the religious landscape. Still, one could say that Norway is marked by a Lutheran approach, where modesty and hard work is a virtue. Turning to a legalistic approach, some cultural values are expressed in the Constitution. According to section 2, our 'values will remain our Christian and humanist heritage'. Furthermore, the Constitution 'shall ensure democracy, a state based on the rule of law and human rights'. Many acts within the health law field contain provisions stating the aims and purposes, which also reflect basic values within this field of law.[19] The individual's right to autonomy, integrity and dignity is frequently used, as well as safeguards the respect for life. On a societal level, the best possible use of resources is often highlighted.

VI. Overview of the Legal System

26. The drafting of a new act will normally start with an expert committee appointed by the government with the mandate of drafting a new act within a given field.[20] The report will be published in the Official Norwegian Reports (abbrev. 'NOU' in Norwegian). There will then be a hearing, normally followed by a proposition for a new act by the government (abbrev. 'Prop. L' in Norwegian, or 'Ot.prp.' prior to 2009). The relevant committee of the Storting will then do their review and make suggestion for alteration. The act will then be subject of debate and voting of the Storting (with a system of two readings, cf. *supra* paragraph 11). In order to

19. *See* Mette Hartlev, *The raison d'être of Nordic Health Law*, in *Nordic Health Law in a European Context: Welfare State Perspectives on Patients' Rights and Biomedicine* 49–66 (Elisabeth Rynning & Mette Hartlev eds, Nijhoff 2012).
20. For an overview of the legislative process, *see* https://www.stortinget.no/en/In-English/About-the-Storting/Legislation (accessed 10 Jul. 2022).

become valid, the government must as a matter of routine sanction the act. Amendments to the act can be made by a swifter procedure, with a hearing initiated by the government followed by a proposition. Members of parliament can also propose amendments. They will initially be reviewed by a parliament committee but submitted to the government if further follow-up is needed.

27. All acts and regulations, as well as case law and other sources are published on 'lovdata.no'.[21] This database is partly free of charge, and all valid acts and regulations can be assessed from this part. A selection of Norwegian laws and regulations translated into foreign languages is accessible online.[22] However, note that only a limited selection is included, and that the translations are unofficial and may be out of date.

28. The legislative supremacy of the Storting is only limited to the constitution (the text and customary principles are equal to the constitution).[23] The courts can review the legislation's conformity with the constitution (*see* paragraph 35 *infra*). While the Constitution is the only legal restriction on the Storting, other instruments play in practice a more important role. As an EEA member the parliament can refuse to include new EU legislation in the EEA agreement. However, a veto could jeopardize the agreement as such. Norway has until now included all new EEA relevant legislation from the EU (Norway takes part in the preparation in the EU bodies but without a formal vote).

29. As part of the Human Rights Act, the European Convention on Human Rights (ECHR) and the following four UN Conventions (with selected protocols) are incorporated into Norwegian legislation:

(1) the International Covenant on Civil and Political Rights;
(2) the International Covenant on Economic, Social and Cultural Rights;
(3) the Convention on the Rights of the Child; and
(4) the Convention on the Elimination of All Forms of Discrimination against Women.

30. The human instruments incorporated by the Human Rights Act have, according to the wording of section 3, supremacy over concurring statutory provisions. The parliament can in principle amend this at a later occasion, but in practice, the incorporated instruments functions as a form of semi-constitutional legislation. The Supreme Court has held that the supremacy effect is not only connected to the wording of the instruments, but that national legislation should yield if they conflict with an interpretation made by the respective supervision bodies (there are several nuances here which cannot be elaborated within the frame of this contribution).

21. *See* the homepage in English at https://lovdata.no/info/information_in_english (accessed 10 Jul. 201 9).
22. *See* https://app.uio.no/ub/ujur/oversatte-lover/english.shtml (accessed 10 Jul. 2022). *See also* links at the Lovdata homepage referred to in previous footnote.
23. *See also supra* n. 9 for sources regarding the cooperation between Norway and the EU.

While the Human Rights Act incorporates selected international instruments en bloc, human rights and international instruments can be incorporated in specific sectors by statutory provisions, or specific instruments can be incorporated as such. Human rights instruments and international law (including customary law) are also relevant to the principle of presumption. Norwegian law is presumed to be in conformity with the country's international obligations. In case of conflict, the relevant Norwegian legislation will as far as possible be interpreted in line with the international obligation. However, the edge starts when the Norwegian legislation is made regardless of international obligation (*see* Rt. 1997 p. 580 relating to the right to strike and different ILO obligations and HR-2016-2554-P, paragraph 70 regarding the interpretation of section 92 of the Constitution). In the field of health law, specific instruments may be of relevance. The Council of Europe Convention on Protection of Human Rights and Dignity of the Human Being with regard to the Application of Biology and Medicine (Oviedo Convention) 4 April 1997 and the UN Convention on the Rights of Persons with Disabilities (13 December 2006) has both played a role in certain cases, *see* examples in paragraphs 263, 282 and 343 *infra*. Regarding the latter, the Supreme Court held in HR-2016-2591-A that a woman who was a psychiatric patient should be deprived of her legal capacity with regard to financial affairs. The provision in the Guardianship Act (2010) section 22, paragraph 2, which allows such intervention, needed to be considered even though it would be contrary to the UN Convention on the Rights of Persons with Disabilities, which has not been incorporated in Norwegian law. The provision in the Guardianship Act was not considered to be contrary to section 102 of the Constitution of Norway or European Convention on Human Rights (ECHR) Article 8.

31. A regulation (Norwegian 'forskrift') is given on the basis of a competence vested in the act to supply the legislation, and even in some cases to deviate from statutory provisions. Normally, regulations are given by the ministries or other public bodies, but in some areas regulations may also be given by private institutions. As delegated legislation, a regulation has to be in conformity with its legal superiors (acts made by parliament and the constitution). The procedural rules regarding legislation are found in the Public Administration Act (PAA) section 6.

32. The Norwegian legal method has, for historical reasons, many similarities with the Danish legal method, and both are inspired and influenced by continental legal thinking, especially from Germany.[24] It is discussed whether the Nordic countries belong to a separate law family or are to be allocated to the continental family.[25] Although Norway never introduced a civil code (as announced in the constitution until the 2014 reform), most parts of the civil law area are regulated by

---

24. For analysis and discussion of Norwegian legal method, *see* Sören Koch & Ingvill Helland (eds), *Nordic and Germanic Legal Methods Contributions to a Dialogue Between Different Legal Cultures, with a Main Focus on Norway and Germany* (Mohr Siebeck 2014) and Morten Kinander, *The View from Within an Analysis and Critique of Legal Realism and Descriptive Jurisprudence* (Fagbokforlaget 2007).
25. Konrad Zweigert & Hein Kötz, *Introduction to Comparative Law* 276–285 (3rd ed., Oxford 1998) regards the Nordic legal systems as a separate law family.

statutory provisions (with tort law as a striking exception). Turning to administrative law, most areas are also covered by legislation (with judicial review as a striking exception). When interpreting statutory provisions, the preparatory works will normally play a vital role. They are both used to identify the purpose and aim of the legislation and to provide guidance to the interpretation of terms and expression used in the act. Especially with rather recent legislation the preparatory works are important due to the lack of other sources. The use of preparatory work can partly be justified by the notion of finding the spirit of the legislator, but it should be emphasized that preparatory works include documents from the whole legislation chain. Normally, the report from the expert committee and the proposition from the ministry are the most comprehensive and will therefore be of greater interest than expression made during the parliamentary procedure.

33. Case law plays a central role in Norwegian legal method, but the influx will vary between different areas of law. Tort law, as well as substantial administrative law, will to a large extent, be case law driven due to limited guidance by the legislation. Case law will also be a core source in areas where disputes frequently reach the courts. A redundant debate is the Supreme Courts use of its own decisions as landmarks and the willingness to deviate from former rulings.

34. Norwegian legal method can be said to be rather pragmatic and solution based. The American legal realism had an impact on prominent scholars adjusting it to Scandinavian legal realism.[26] Value-based assessments of the best result of the disputes will play a major role if the text of the relevant provision is unclear or if relevant sources are pointing in different directions. This provides flexibility for the judges, but at the same time it can be difficult for the actors to foresee their judicial position. This pragmatism can perhaps be connected to the social values. The Norwegian society is a small community where values to a large extent are common. Combined with a high degree of confidence – in this case to the judiciary – it is an acceptance that courts will find the best solution for the individual case. However, it must be emphasized that this explanation is rather simplistic and it should also be added that the contemporary tendency moves towards paying more attention to the wording of the provisions and more consequences-oriented interpretations.

35. There are three levels of jurisdiction in Norway.[27] There are currently twenty-three District Courts (down from sixty-six in 2016) and six High Courts. As with the municipalities and regions, there is an ongoing process of reversing the previous reforms regarding reductions in the number of district courts. The Supreme Court in Oslo was established by the 1814 Constitution (until then there was a joint Supreme Court for Denmark and Norway) and began its activities in 1815. The courts handle both civil and criminal cases, and there are no special administrative

---

26. *See* Jes Bjarup, *The Philosophy of Scandinavian Legal Realism*, 18 Ratio Juris 1–15 (2005) and Jaakko Husa, Kimmo Nuotio & Heikki Pihlajamäki (eds), *Nordic Law – Between Tradition and Dynamism* (Intersentia 2007).
27. For a presentation of the Norwegian Courts Administration and the judicial system, *see* https://www.domstol.no (accessed 10 Jul. 2022, the process of translating selected information into English in ongoing).

courts. In many areas different boards are established which may have procedural guarantees like a court (*see* examples in paragraph 203 (patient injuries) and paragraph 311 (child care cases)). However, such decisions can be challenged before the ordinary courts.

36. The Supreme Court has twenty justices headed by the Chief Justice.[28] The main role of the Supreme Court is to ensure 'uniformity, clarity and development of the law'. Appeals from the High Courts are reviewed by the Appeals Selection Committee (three judges), and only a limited number of cases are decided each year. Normally, judgments are delivered after an oral hearing by a chamber composed of five judges. Important cases may be decided by a grand chamber (eleven judges) or by the court in plenary (all judges). In 2021, the Supreme Court heard in chambers fifty-nine civil cases and twenty-nine criminal cases (except two, all after an oral hearing). In grand chamber, one civil case and one criminal case were heard, and one civil case was heard in plenary. A full text of judgments and decisions with grounds from the Appeals is published on the court's website, while the summary of judgments by the Supreme Court is available in English (dating back to 2000) and a selection of rulings is translated into English. Until 2015, judgments were referred to by the page in the report book of the Supreme Court (Norsk Retstidende, Rt.), but after the termination of the printed version, they are referred to according to their case number, followed by a letter indicating whether a plenary (P), grand chamber (S), chamber (A) or by the appeals board (U).

37. The 1814 Constitution did not contain any provisions regarding judicial review of administrative decisions. Despite the lack of constitutional legal basis, the Supreme Court shortly after 1815 took the position that the courts can review the legality of administrative decisions and to some extent also can review the administrative discretion.[29] The principle of legality is now expressed in the Constitution, cf. section 113 ('Infringement of the authorities against the individual must be founded on the law.'). Additionally, judicial review of administrative decision concerning deprivation of liberty – including confinement in psychiatric institution – is now guaranteed by the Constitution, cf. section 94, second paragraph. Regarding judicial review of medical matters, health law is part of administrative law, the review by the courts is normally limited to a control of legality as well as to assessing whether the procedural requirements are fulfilled. The courts can also declare a decision for invalid if the decision is based on erroneous facts. The review of the administrative discretion is limited, although the threshold is not so high that the control is absent (*see infra* paragraph 43 and Rt. 1990 p. 874 for an example from health law).

---

28. *See* https://www.domstol.no/en/supremecourt/ (accessed 10 Jul. 2022).
29. *See* Anneken Kari Sperr, *Verwaltungsrechtsschutz in Deutschland und Norwegen: eine vergleichende Studie zur gerichtlichen Kontrolle von Verwaltungsentscheidungen (Judicial Review in Germany and Norway: A Comparative Study of Court Supervision of Administrative Decisions)* (Nomos 2009).

38. The courts have also established the rule of constitutional review, where the courts have the competence to assess whether statutory provisions by the Storting are in accordance with the Constitution (*see supra* paragraph 29 regarding international human rights instruments and the Human Rights Act). The courts' competence of constitutional review is now guaranteed by the Constitution, cf. section 89. The intensity of this scrutiny has varied. Currently, the Supreme Court appears to be rather active, where the reform of the Constitution seems to have fertilized the development.

39. As stated earlier (*see supra* paragraph 1) Jan Mayen and Spitsbergen (Svalbard) have a particular legal position. Besides acts relating to criminal matters and civil law, legislation does not apply in these areas unless dictated in the relevant acts. Previously, such provisions were rather rare in the field of health law. By regulation of 22 June 2015 No. 747, most health law regulations are now applicable of Svalbard and Jan Mayen.

§2. General Description of the Healthcare System

I. General Review of the Healthcare System

40. As in many other countries the earlier legal regulation in the medical field has mostly been on institutions (hospitals) and the medical doctors. A presentation of some milestones of the legislative development will follow under next headline. The legislation is on the legal surface,[30] and in many areas acts made by the parliament are merely a confirmation of developments that have already taken place and where the driving forces are other than the legislative process. Many health law issues are closely linked to budgets, especially in countries like Norway where health services to a large extent are public-funded. Consequently, major health reforms will normally require sufficient funding, and the parliament has been a main engine in the built-up of the Norwegian health system. The political processes are of course complex, and combined with a lot of other factors. Some of them will be topics for discussion in the following paragraphs.

41. All the three levels of administration are involved in the distribution of health services (*see* paragraph 13). The state is responsible for specialized health services, like hospitals, as the owner of the four regional health enterprises. According to the Health Authorities and Health Trust Act, the regional health enterprises do not by themselves own institutions, but they can own health enterprises, running hospitals, etc. or buy services from private providers. The municipalities are responsible for primary health services. The regions (counties) have the responsibility for dental healthcare (a reform transferring this responsibility to the municipalities was decided in 2017, but later reversed).

30. Compare Kaarlo Tuori, *Critical Legal Positivism* 147–196 (Ashgate 2002) and his division into three layers of law: 'the surface of the law', 'the legal culture' and 'the deep structure of modern law'.

42. Some of the revisions of the legislation have been caused by major events. 'Reitgjerdet' was a former prison in the mid-Norway which in the beginning of the 1960s was converted into a psychiatric hospital for, especially, dangerous patients. The conditions and over use of coercive measures were discussed in public, especially after a doctor escaped with a patient. A public investigation was carried out led by a Supreme Court judge, sharply criticizing the conditions for the patients. Many patients were given economic compensation after recommendation by a board established by the government. Some patients also successfully claimed for compensation under ordinary lawsuits. In Rt. 1987 p. 1495, the Supreme Court held that detention without fulfilling the condition for compulsory confinement should be compensated on objective grounds (no requirement of negligence). The 'Reitgjerdet' case did not have a direct impact on the legislation. The committee drafting a new act for psychiatric patients ended up in a drawer in the ministry,[31] but the discussions in the report functioned as fertilizer for the ongoing development of patients' rights. Today, mass media plays a major role in addressing shortcomings of the health system and has a direct impact on the political agenda. This may be a disadvantage for vulnerable groups without a solid standing in media.

43. The Norwegian Supreme Court has had some health law cases which have been groundbreaking, and the 'Reitgjerdet' case is already mentioned. Another milestone case was Rt. 1977 p. 1035. A former patient initiated proceedings in order to have access to his own medical record. The hospital denied access claiming that the medical record was an internal document containing working notes from the doctor. Access to the patients' own medical record was at the time not regulated in the legislation. The Supreme Court held that the patient was entitled to his medical records. The judgment is based on 'general principles of law' and the court openly made a balance of the involved interests. Rt. 1990 p. 874 concerned a handicapped woman living at home supported by her parents. The municipality severely diminished her home care and social services due to increased costs. The background was a revision of the system of reimbursement from the state to the municipalities. The decision to reduce services was explicitly made with reference to economic situation, and it aimed to 'encourage' the patient to apply for a stay at an institution (then the responsibility of the county). In their judgment, the Supreme Court held that the current legislation entitled the patients to services from the municipality. Regarding the content of the right to health services, the Supreme Court was reluctant to go into the details and the administrative discretion, but clearly stated that there exists a minimum standard that no municipality could go below, even given consideration to their financial situation. The decision was therefore declared void. The judgment from the Supreme Court has been comprehensively discussed in the legal doctrine (mainly in Norwegian), and reference to the judgment has also been made by the legislator in preparatory works.

44. Traditionally health services were seen as a part of administrative law. In the 1970s, health issues were addressed in the legal doctrine and health law (together

---

31. NOU 1988:8 *Lov om psykisk helsevern uten eget samtykke (Act Relating to Psychiatric Care without Consent).*

with social law) was established as a separate discipline.[32] The late professor Asbjørn Kjønstad (1943–2015) was a pioneer, thus supported by many other scholars (*see also* the selected bibliography *infra*). An important aspect of the discourse in the legal theory was the patients' perspective inspired by the critical law movement. Health law is now part of the curriculum at all three institutions awarding a master's degree in law (compulsory part in Oslo and eligible Tromsø and Bergen).

45. The development of health law has traditionally been rather national oriented, though inspired by legislation in other parts of Europe, especially the Nordic neighbouring countries. Historically, the Nordic countries have had a close collaboration when preparing new legislation, but the cooperation in forms of joint expert groups had its peak before the evolvement of health legislation. A more recent trend is the impact of different instruments of an international origin. This could stem from UN bodies, WHO, the Council of Europe and the EU. Relevant instruments and their impact on the legislation will be referred to in the appropriate field.

II. Regulation of the Healthcare System

46. The earliest forms of written regulation from the medieval period contain no provision of what we today would call health law, although having provisions on health-related issues. The earliest form of health law can be traced back to pharmacies, but the first legislation came in the mid-nineteenth century. Milestone acts are the regulations of mental patients (1848) and public health (1860). The emergence of a healthcare system is closely connected to labour legislation, providing industry workers – and their family members – access to health services. The Health Insurance Act (1909) provided access to medical doctors and hospitals for workers, their spouses and younger children (under the age of 15). About 1 million of the then population of 2.4 million were covered by the act.[33]

47. The earliest act regulating the medical profession was the act relating to public doctors (1912), but the first act targeting physicians was enacted in 1927. This act on the rights and duties of medical doctors laid down some core obligations:[34]

- The obligation of medical confidentiality (this duty was already established in other provisions, such as the Criminal Code), cf. section 14.

32. *See* Asbjørn Kjønstad & Aslak Syse, *The Growth of Patients' Rights in Norway*, in *Patient's Rights: Informed Consent, Access and Equality* 255–278 (Lotta Westerhäll & Charles Phillips eds, Nerenius and Santérus 1994) and Asbjørn Kjønstad, *The Development of Patients' Rights in Norway*, in *Nordic Health Law in a European Context: Welfare State Perspectives on Patients' Rights and Biomedicine* 107–121 (Elisabeth Rynning & Mette Hartlev eds, Nijhoff 2012).
33. Asbjørn Kjønstad, *Helserett – pasienter og helsearbeideres rettsstilling (Health Law – The Legal Protection of Patients and Health Personnel)* 79 (2d ed., Gyldendal 2007).
34. Asbjørn Kjønstad, *Helserett – pasienter og helsearbeideres rettsstilling (Health Law – The Legal Protection of Patients and Health Personnel)* 79 (2d ed., Gyldendal 2007).

- The obligation to provide health services in emergency situations (combined with a corresponding entitlement for the patient to emergency health services in such situations), cf. section 7.
- The obligation to sparseness when providing health services (both to limit the public expenses and to minimize the fees for the patients), cf. section 13.
- The obligation to report births, deaths and infectious diseases to the authorities, cf. section 11.
- The obligation to make and keep medical reports, cf. section 12.

48. This act on the rights and duties of medical doctors laid was given simultaneously as the act on the rights and duties of dentists. Later on, acts were given targeting other groups of health personnel, such as physiotherapists (1956), nurses (1960), psychologists (1973) and other health personnel (1974). Midwives were regulated by a separate act already in 1898. The acts regulating other groups of health personnel was less extensive than the acts on medical doctors and dentist, although all of them stating the obligation of medical confidentiality.

49. The act relating to mental patients was replaced in 1961 by the Mental Health Care Act. Basically, the 1961 act was a modernization, without any major changes compared with previous regulations. The first act relating to hospitals was given in 1969. This act contained mainly provisions on the administration of hospitals (planning, organization and funding). Together with the Mental Health Care Act, the Hospital Act was vital for the built-up of the public, specialized healthcare system. Although mainly addressing the administration, the regulations also contained provisions with elements of patients' rights. A pioneering provision of the Hospital Act was section 6 obliging hospitals to admit patients in an emergency situation (from 1981 also a similar provision in the Mental Health Care Act). According to these provisions the institution was responsible, not the medical professional (such as under the act on the rights and duties of medical doctors). In the same period the Public Administrative Act was introduced (1967), being the first general regulation of administrative law, replacing and streamlining many procedural requirements in various specialized acts (including the health sector).

50. In the 1970s, the parliament introduced three important acts on various medical interventions. The Transplant Act required written consent prior to the use of organs or other biological material. The act also included provisions for hospital autopsies and the donation of bodies. The Abortion Act (1975) regulated termination of pregnancy (cf. paragraph 330 *infra*). From 1977, the women had the right to self-determination before the twelfth week of pregnancy. The Sterilisation Act was introduced in 1977 stipulating as a general rule that such intervention could only be carried out after the request of the person concerned and if the person is over the age of 25 (cf. paragraph 336 *infra*). The act also included provisions on castration.

51. In 1980, the acts relating to rights and duties of medical doctors and dentists were both replaced. The different provisions were modernized, but some new rights were also introduced: the right to information, the right to access to one's own medical record (already established by case law, cf. *supra* paragraph 45) and the right to participation. A general provision on the patients' right to self-determination or to consent was not introduced. In 1985, the parliament also introduced a new Midwife Act.

52. The Act relating to Municipal Health Care Services was introduced in 1982. This act was mainly addressing the administration of the primary healthcare system but also contained a provision regarding access to health services (*see supra* paragraph 45 regarding Rt. 1990 p. 874 and the patient's right to health services). The public dental health system was established in some municipalities at the beginning of the twentieth century. The Dental Care Act of 1983 had a similar structure as the Act relating to Municipal Health Care Services. However, access to public dental services was limited to minors and selected vulnerable groups (elderly and mentally handicapped). The vast majority of the population is responsible for taking care of their own dental health out of their own pocket.

53. A major revision of the Norwegian Health Law took place in 1999. The reform was partly fertilized by the growing discussion in the legal doctrine of health law issues. Four acts were part of the reform: the Patients' Rights Act (the title was revised in 2011, now also including 'users' of care services, but the former title will be used here), the Health Personnel Act (HPA), the Mental Health Care Act and the Specialized Health Care Act. The Patients' Rights Act (PRA) contains provisions according to its title. Some of the rights that were already found in the former act relating to medical doctors are transferred to the new act, like medical confidentiality, but the different rights are regulated more in detail. The PRA also contains provision without predecessors in the general legislation, like the right to consent. The Mental Health Care Act regulates specialized care for patients with mental illnesses, governing both access to psychiatric institutions (voluntary and compulsory confinement) and the rules during the stay. The PRA also applies to patients in psychiatric institutions, cf. the Mental Health Care Act section 1-5. The HPA regulates the rights and duties of health personnel. Instead of the previous legal regime of separate acts for each profession, the new act covers all professions listed in the act. Some of the rights and duties of the health personnel also have direct implications for the patients, like the provisions on medical confidentiality, cf. HPA sections 21–34. The Specialized Health Care Act replaced the former Hospital Act. It covers hospitals and other institutions (e.g., for alcoholics and drug addicts) as well as specialized health services, cf. section 2-1 regarding the different services. The organizations of the public hospitals are regulated in the Health Authorities and Health Trust Act.

54. The responsibilities of the municipalities, both regarding healthcare and care services, are governed by the Health and Care Services Act (2011). The Health and Care Services Act replaced the former Act relating to Municipal Health Care Services in 1982. It contains common rules for both health and care services at the local level. The rights of the patients are found in the PRA, although some of the provisions in the Health and Care Services Act have an impact on the legal position of the patients. In addition to the acts already presented, the parliament has also passed acts covering patient injury, medical research, etc. This legislation will be referred to in the text below.

55. The Constitution from 1814 did not from the beginning contain provision relating to healthcare. However, general requirements could also have an impact on health law, like the prohibition on retroactive legislation and the protection of property (*see* Rt. 1996 p. 1415 and Rt. 1996 p. 1440 on social rights). As part of the bicentennial of the Constitution, the protection of human rights was reformed. The committee preparing the amendments had proposed that the state should promote the populations' health and secure the right to necessary healthcare.[35] In the parliament there were not a sufficient majority for including economic and social rights, and the proposal fell.

III. Financing of the Healthcare System

56. The Norwegian health system is to a large extent public funded.[36] It is based on a general coverage for those residing in the country and access to health services is normally not linked to the position as an employee. The regional health enterprises are directly funded by the state budget. A large part of their income is dependent on activity, where the different diagnoses are evaluated and the enterprises are paid according to this. The regional health enterprises can provide services either through their under enterprises or they can buy services from other providers, being both private and public (entities from other regions), or even abroad. The use of private providers has been limited and is indeed an issue of political debate, but gradually the private institutions have become more important. However, most patients are treated in public hospitals. The municipalities – as well as the counties – are partly funded by local taxation, but they are dependent on state funding. Most of the funding is giving as block grant (based on populations, etc.), instead of earmarked posts for specific activity, cf. Health Care and Services Act section 11-5.

57. Since the municipalities are responsible for primary healthcare and the regional health enterprises are responsible for specialized healthcare, conflicts may arise from time to time between the levels of organization relating to who is responsible for the patient. Health and Care Services Act section 6-1 establishes as a legal obligation that the regional health enterprises and the municipalities should enter an agreement of cooperation, and also stipulates the content of such agreements. Municipalities that cannot take care of patients, who have been treated at the hospital and are awaiting a stay in a municipal health or care institution, may be subject to cover the expenses of the regional health enterprise.

35. Dok. 16 (2001–2012) Rapport til Stortingets presidentskap fra Menneskerettighetsutvalget om menneskerettigheter i Grunnloven (Report to the Storting's Presidium from the Human Rights Committee Regarding the Protection of Human Rights in the Constitution).

36. Wolf Sauters et al. (eds), *The Law and Policy of Healthcare Financing. An International Comparison of Models and Outcomes* (Edward Elgar Publishing 2019), which also includes a chapter on the Norwegian model.

58. Every person residing in Norway is a member of the National Insurance Scheme, cf. the National Insurance Act. The National Insurance Act is primarily regulating different kinds of cash benefits (like pensions and unemployment subsidies). However, in some specific areas health law provisions refer to the National Insurance Scheme and the membership here, cf. Health and Care Services Act section 11-5 and National Insurance Act Chapter 5. Some entitlements require that the person has been a member of the National Insurance Scheme for a certain time. The National Insurance Scheme is partly funded by taxation and partly funded through the state budget.

59. The regulation of payments from patients is not found in a single provision but depends on the actual form of treatment. According to Health and Care Services Act section 11-2 the municipality can charge the patient if such payment is stipulated in an act by parliament or regulations by the ministry. For a visit to a general practitioner, there is a small fee (from NOK 223, approx. EUR 22), with exemptions for different groups (like children, etc.) and conditions (like infectious diseases). Patients living in an institution, i.e., for the elderly, can be charged a fee up to 85% of their income, with the actual expenses as a threshold. Hospital treatment is free of charge, while policlinic visits and visits to a specialist are subject to a fee (NOK 375, approx. EUR 37), with exemptions for different groups (like children, etc.) and conditions (infectious diseases). There is a maximum annual threshold for fees paid on primary and specialized healthcare (NOK 2921, approx. EUR 290), cf. National Insurance Act section 5-3. Patients falling outside the coverage, for example, tourists not covered by EEA legislation or irregular migrants, are subject to the full cost of the healthcare, cf. Specialist Health Care Act section 5-3.[37] However, the institution cannot claim payment in advance, so patients in these situations will have access to emergency healthcare with reimbursement claims afterwards. If so, the patient is subject to reimbursement of the full cost of treatment.

Dental care falls outside the public coverage, unless the need is considered to be a disease, cf. National Insurance Act section 5-6. Some groups are covered by the public dental care system, like young people (under the age of 20 years old), mentally handicapped, residents in healthcare institutions and alcoholics and drug addicts (under certain conditions).

IV. Access to Healthcare Services: Prioritization

60. Historically, access to the healthcare services was based on the discretion of the providers, which could be obliged to help according to their ethical codes. Gradually, the issue has been subject to regulations and today it is one of the core elements of patients' entitlements (case law has also been influential, *see* Rt. 1990 p. 874). Current legislation differs between 'emergency healthcare' and 'necessary

37. *See* Karl Harald Søvig, *Provision of Health Services to Irregular Migrants with a Special Focus on Children,* 18 Eur. J. Health L. 43–54 (2011) and Marry-Anne Karlsen, *Precarious Inclusion. Irregular Migration, Practice of Care, and State B/Ordering in Norway* (PhD Dissertation, University of Bergen 2015).

healthcare'. Everyone has the right to 'emergency healthcare' from the municipality and from the specialized health services, cf. respectively PRA section 2-1a, first paragraph and section 2-1b, first paragraph, *see also* HPA section 7 (*see infra* paragraph 100 regarding the obligations of health personnel) and the Health and Care Services Act section 3-5 (regarding the obligation of the municipality). Additionally, everyone has the right to 'necessary healthcare' from to municipality and from the specialized health services, cf. respectively PRA section 2-1a, second paragraph and section 2-1b, second paragraph. The obligation to provide necessary healthcare is also stipulated in the Specialized Health Care Act section 3-1.

61. Both 'emergency healthcare' and 'necessary healthcare' are legal standards which leave a room for interpretations, but they are established as operable expressions within the medical community. In cases of emergency care the need for intervention is more acute than in cases of necessary healthcare, but it should be added that about 67% of admittance into hospitals are based on emergency care.[38] In both cases the approach is two-folded: assessment of the condition, and intervention if the requirements are fulfilled. Turning to necessary healthcare from the specialized healthcare services, this approach is also written into the provisions. According to PRA section 2-1b, third paragraph the patient's condition shall be examined and the provider shall set a time limit for when healthcare should latest be provided. For some conditions specific deadlines are set by regulation. If healthcare is not provided within the deadline, the patient is entitled to healthcare, also from private providers or from providers outside the country, cf. PRA section 2-1b, fourth paragraph. If necessary healthcare cannot be provided due to lack of adequate treatment within the country, the patient is entitled to treatment abroad, cf. PRA section 2-1b, fifth paragraph

62. The legislation regarding access to healthcare has been amended several times and is closely linked to redundant debates regarding prioritization.[39] A part of this debate is the access to health services for non-members of the welfare state, like irregular migrants.[40] When it comes to health services and EEA law, both the Directive on the Application of Patients' Rights in Cross-Border Healthcare (2011/24/EC) and Regulation (EC) No. 883/2004 2004 on the coordination of social security systems are EEA relevant. The directive and the regulation are implemented in the national legislation by PRA section 2-4a, which was introduced in 2019 (*see also* regulation of 22 November 2010 No. 1466). Regulation 883/2004 – with subsequent amendments – is as such implemented as domestic regulation (22 June 2012

38. Norwegian Directorate of Health (IS-2711), p. 1 (2018). The figures are from 2017 (somatic healthcare).
39. *See*: NOU 2014:12 *Åpent og rettferdig – prioriteringer i helsetjenesten (Openness and Justice – Prioritization within Health Services*) and NOU 2018: 16 *Det viktigste først – Prinsipper for prioritering i den kommunale helse- og omsorgstjenesten og for offentlig finansierte tannhelsetjenester* (The most important first – Principles of prioritization in the municipal health and care services and for publicly funded dental health care services).
40. *See* Synnøve K. Bendixsen, Christine M. Jacobsen & Karl Harald Søvig (eds), *Eksepsjonell velferd? irregulære immigranter i det norske velferdssamfunnet* (*Exceptional Welfare? Irregular Migrants in the Norwegian Welfare Society*) (Gyldendal 2015).

No. 585) with supremacy over specific conflicting statutory legislation, including the National Security Act, but not the Patient's Rights Act. The basic requirement is that healthcare provided in another EU/EEA Member State is only covered insofar as the patient would have been entitled to care according to national legislation. The patient can in such cases either have the expenses reimbursed or require a prior authorization regarding whether the treatment would be covered and the maximum amount that will be reimbursed.[41] Additionally, the patient is entitled to be reimbursed for necessary healthcare during temporary stays and for planned healthcare in other EEA States if the healthcare is not provided within a reasonable time in Norway. PRA section 2-4a also entitles patient for healthcare abroad, beyond the EEA area, if the patient is entitled to necessary healthcare from the specialist health service according to PRA section 2-1 b and there is no offer in the country or the healthcare abroad is documented to be more effective than the healthcare offered by the public sector in Norway. Expenditure on healthcare that has been decided not to be introduced in Norway is not covered (cf. the Specialized Health Services Act section 4-4). In exceptional cases the patient can also be given experimental or exploitable treatment abroad (also outside EEA) (cf. regulation of 1 December 2000 section 3).

63. The EFTA Surveillance Authority (ESA) monitors compliance with EEA rules in Iceland, Liechtenstein and Norway. ESA in 2019 decided to refer Norway to the EFTA Court over Norwegian rules that restrict people's rights to seek hospital treatment in other EEA States. The decision to refer Norway to the EFTA Court followed an infringement procedure launched in 2014 after ESA had received numerous complaints about the Norwegian restrictions. ESA sent in May 2022 a supplementary letter of formal notice to Norway over national rules that restrict people's rights to seek hospital treatment in other EEA States.[42] The supplementary letter of formal notice is being sent following new information received by ESA while preparing its application to the EFTA Court as well as changes to Norwegian law after ESA decided to refer Norway to the EFTA Court (cf. *supra* regarding PRA section 2-4a, amended in 2021). During its case work, ESA reviewed more than 200 administrative decisions, which according to ESA revealed that EEA rules had in practice not been applied correctly or considered. In ESA's view, the Norwegian Patients' Rights Act does not meet the requirements of EEA rules in a number of areas, for example:

(1) The EEA Social Security Regulation has not been implemented correctly in Norway when it comes to patients' rights to receive treatment abroad, as EEA law is not given precedence over the Norwegian Patients' Rights Act.
(2) The conditions under the Patients' Rights Act for the right to treatment abroad are too strict. These include a requirement that the patient provides documentation that the treatment abroad is more effective than the public treatment offered in Norway.

41. *See* https://www.helsenorge.no/en/treatment-abroad/ (accessed 10 Jul. 2022).
42. Case No. 72376, Decision No. 113/22/COL.

(3) Where a patient is denied authorization to receive treatment abroad by Norway, the Patients' Rights Act system for handling complaints limits the possibility for relevant appeal bodies to apply EEA law the correct way. In addition, EEA law is in practice rarely used or applied correctly by the relevant appeal bodies.
(4) The Norwegian rules lack the clarity, precision and degree of legal certainty required by EEA rules. This is, for example, because the Patients' Rights Act includes rules that are in conflict with EEA law, making it difficult for patients to understand and exercise their rights.

64. The case is still pending.

§3. Sources of Medical Law

65. Contemporary medical law is to a large extent developed by legislation, which in many cases only can have the indented effect if supported by sufficient budget funding. Historically, the legislation was more fragmented (*see also supra* paragraphs 49 ff). The trend in recent years has been a legalization where previous case law based areas (e.g., compensation for patient injuries) or unregulated fields have been subject to regulation by statutory provisions. The legislation has also been rather frequently updated and amended, which have led to a rather complex legal landscape.

66. The starting point when solving legal disputes will be the text and the established meaning of the terms and words used. As in other Nordic countries (*see also supra* paragraph 33), the preparatory work is an important source when interpreting and applying statutory provisions. The impact of preparatory work will depend on a number of factors, where the existence of other relevant sources is a core element. Many health law issues will have to be solved without guidance in case law, which increases the influence of the preparatory works. Another factor will be the societal changes. In some areas, like biotechnology, these have taken place so fast that the guidance given in preparatory work could not necessarily be taken as today's opinion of the legislator. It should also be noted that in some situations the signals given in the preparatory work will be contradicting or unclear, and the impact will of course also depend on the clarity of the guidance provided by the legislator.

67. In some parts of health law, court decisions have played an important role. Many of the most well-known judgments have concerned issues where the legislation is unclear, and where the Supreme Court has solved the matter in a kind of innovative way, often involving value-based assessment, which has been applauded by legal doctrine (Rt. 1990 p. 874 concerning right to healthcare is often used as example, cf. *supra* paragraph 44). In some cases the Supreme Court has even come to conclusions that in practice alters the legal situation and is setting the statutory provisions aside (Rt. 1977 p. 1035 concerning access to medical records is often used as an example, cf. paragraph 43). Most judgments are still not groundbreaking, but are bit-by-bit moving and adjusting the legal borders, often in interplay with the legislation (as with patient compensation).

68. In legal theory there is reluctance towards accepting circulars as a legal source, especially if the viewpoint in the circulars limits the citizen's legal position. The ministry has the ability to suggest amendments in the legislation and should therefore not use circulars as a form of backdoor without the public debate and vote in the parliament. However, in practice, circulars play an important role, and they are often compiling legal sources in a way that makes them useful for health personnel in their everyday life. Regarding prioritization circular has in practice been important. The Directorate of Health has issued guidelines for prioritization within thirty-three medical fields, which plays a crucial role in everyday clinical life. The purpose is to achieve equal treatment within all regional health enterprises.

69. When the Supreme Court is reasoning their judgments, they refer to legal doctrine from time to time, but one could not say that legal doctrine is an important source of law. However, the legal doctrine has been taking part in the development of health law as an academic discipline, which has also influenced the legislator. Many scholars also have an impact on the legislation in their role as members of expert committees drafting new legislation or in other positions when acting as experts.

70. Value-based assessment plays a significant role within the Norwegian legal method.[43] The values are often extracted from the objects of the legislation as stipulated in a purpose section or the purposes elaborated in the preparatory work. In other situation the court develops them. This approach has raised critique, especially where the courts only refer to the assessment, without detailing the factors taken into consideration. The prevision mentioned Supreme Court decision concerning access to medical records is a striking example of an open and explicit value-based approach (Rt. 1977 p. 1035). The value-based assessments are often rather focused on the individual case and the outcome. It has been discussed whether this quite pragmatic approach can be linked to a rather homogeneous society which to a large degree can identify common values.

71. The so-called *Wound* case from the field of health law that can illustrate some aspects of the methodological approach (Rt. 2010 p. 612, *see also* paragraph 239). The patient had several wounds, which needed frequent changes of bandages, but the patient – which was competent to consent – objected to this care. The core of the matter was whether the nursing home could change bandages and care for his wounds without the consent of the patient. The relevant provision did not provide sufficient legal basis for involuntary intervention. Based on the pressing need for care, combined with an accumulation of the legal basis in which each was insufficient, the majority of the Supreme Court held that intervention was justified. This is

43. *See* Morten Kinander, *The View from Within an Analysis and Critique of Legal Realism and Descriptive Jurisprudence* (Fagbokforlaget 2007).

a rather pragmatic approach, which can be contrasted with the minority. Even though recognizing that the lack of legal basis put the nursing home in a difficult situation, the minority held that it should not be the task of the judiciary to repair shortcomings within the core field of the principle of legality. Compulsory interventions should only take place in situations prescribed by the legislator.

Part I. The Medical Profession

Chapter 1. Access to the Medical Profession

§1. Training of Physicians

72. The medical degree programme leads to the cand.med. degree. The duration of the programme is six years. Four universities in Norway offer the medical degree programme. Previously, the candidate had to undergo a practical part ('turnus') to achieve authorization. The practical part contained twelve months of service in a hospital and six months of service in the municipal healthcare service, where the candidates were located by lot.[44] The latter has been important to secure sufficient coverage for physicians in rural areas, and in practice many of them worked alone with only limited supervision and follow-up.

73. The system was revised in 2012 through amendments to the relevant regulations. A rising number of Norwegian students taking a medical degree abroad, combined with more physicians from a common European market, had led to waiting times of up to one year before starting the practical training. Practical training is no longer a requirement for authorization, although most physicians will undergo practical training. Physicians with authorization, but without practical training, can take various positions as long as the employer facilitates professional conduct. However, certain positions requires practical training or to be under sufficient guidance, for example, in order to claim reimbursement from the National Insurance Scheme. For physicians with a degree from an EU/EEA member country, the Norwegian Directorate of Health has made a list on whether they can apply for direct authorization, depending on whether the education contains practical training.

§2. Manpower Planning

74. Health personnel holding an authorization or licence shall notify the municipality or regional health enterprise upon opening, taking over or entering a practice governed by the HPA, cf. HPA section 18.

75. The responsibility for manpower planning within the public health system is divided between primary and specialized health services. The municipality has a

44. *See* circular IS-6/2015 from the Norwegian Directorate of Health regarding practical training.

legal obligation to ensure that people who reside in the municipality are offered the necessary health (and care) services, cf. Health and Care Services Act section 3-1, first paragraph. In order to comply with this responsibility the municipality must, among other things, offer the following, cf. Health and Care Services Act section 3-2:

- health-promoting and preventive services (No. 1);
- pregnancy and postnatal care services (No. 2);
- assistance in the event of accident and other acute situations (No. 3), including accident and emergency units (litra a), 24-hour emergency medical response (litra b), emergency medical services (litra c) and psycho-social alertness and follow-up (litra d);
- assessment, diagnosis and treatment, including the regular GP scheme (No. 4);
- social, psychosocial and medical habilitation and rehabilitation (No. 5);
- other health and care services (No. 6); and
- daily activity offers to person residing at home suffering from dementia (No. 7).

76. The regional health enterprises have a legal obligation to ensure that persons who reside or stay in the health region are offered specialized healthcare inside and outside the institution, cf. Specialized Health Care Act section 2-1a. This responsibility includes:

- hospital services (No. 1);
- medical laboratory and radiological services (No. 2);
- acute medical alertness (No. 3);
- medical emergency call services, air ambulance services and ambulance services by car or by boat if necessary (No. 4);
- interdisciplinary specialized treatment for alcoholics and drug addicts (No. 5);
- transport for examination or treatment in the municipal health and care services (No. 6); and
- transport of health personnel (No. 7).

77. In order to fulfil their obligation, the regional health enterprises and the municipality have a leeway within the boundaries set by the statutory provisions. Some tasks may be carried out by private contractors with an agreement with the public entities.

I. Freedom of Establishment

78. There is a general freedom of establishment in Norway. However, since the health sector to a large extent is public funded, most physicians are either employed by public entities or have an agreement with public entities. There is an increase of physicians working outside the public sector, where the full cost of the treatment is paid by the patients or financed through the patients' insurance. A growing field is different forms of cosmetic surgery.

§3. LICENSING OF PHYSICIANS

I. General Practitioners

79. The Norwegian Registration Authority for Health Personnel is delegated the responsibility for approving physicians as well as other professions within the health sector, cf. HPA section 53. *Authorization* represents a full and permanent approval, while *licence* imposes one or more limitations with respect to duration, independent or supervised practice/training, etc., cf. HPA sections 48, 48a and 49. The main purpose of the system of authorization and licensing is to safeguard patients' safety and contribute to the trust of health personnel in the general public. Additionally, the system must provide the applicants with a fair assessment of their skills. The provisions were revised in 2015 in order to clarify the rules and codify the administrative practice (law of 19 June 2015 No. 59).[45]

80. Physicians educated in Norway – or physicians educated abroad if they meet certain conditions – and having completed their practical training are entitled to be granted an authorization, unless the person 'is not considered unfit for the profession', cf. HPA section 48a, second paragraph, litra a). In position providing services to children or mentally handicapped, health personnel must submit a police certificate (indicating violation of specific provision in the Criminal Code), cf. HPA section 20a.

81. There is a maximum age requirement of 80 years, which was lifted from 75 years (amendment by law of 19 June 2015 No. 61). The age limit was raised with reference to the general policy of inclusion of elderly in the working society and as well as the EU policy of 'Active ageing and solidarity between generations'.[46] The revised age limit was introduced against the advice of the Norwegian Board of Health Supervision. In the preparatory paper, the ministry discussed to substitute the age limit with a system of recertification, which is used in several other countries.

82. In 2014, 161 physicians over 75 years were given licence.[47] The age limit to act as a physician must be separated from the age limit for the position in which the physician may be employed, which is regulated by law or agreement.

83. Physicians over the age of 80 years can apply for licence, cf. regulation on licensing of healthcare personnel (21 December 2000 No. 1379) sections 6–9. The regulation contains several conditions, *inter alia,* whether the applicant is suited to continue his/hers medical practice. The ability to be medical updated is of special relevance when assessing the application. The licence period – with the possibility for prolongation – is one year. The licence can be given with limitations, for

45. Prop. 99 L (2014–2015), *Endringer i helsepersonelloven mv. (vilkår for autorisasjon) (Amendments to the Health Personnel Act, Etc. (Requirements for Authorization)).*
46. Prop. 74 (2014–2015), *Endringer i helsepersonelloven mv. (endring av aldersgrensen for bortfall av helsepersonells autorisasjon mv. fra 75 til 80 år (Amendments to the Health Personnel Act, Etc. (Amendment of the Age Limit for Withdrawal of Authorization from 75 to 80 years)).*
47. Prop. 74 (2014–2015), table 3.1.

example, when it comes to prescriptions or patients (e.g., only treating family members). Licence is not necessary for teaching or to act as a medical expert. Most applications from physicians for a licence are granted, although sometimes with limitations. From 2010 to 2013, only two were turned down.[48]

84. Physicians educated in other EU/EEA Member States with a diploma will be entitled to authorization in Norway, cf. Directive 2005/36/EC on the recognition of professional qualifications. The directive is implemented by regulation on authorization, licensing and approval as a specialist for health personnel with occupational qualifications from other EEA countries or Switzerland (8 October 2008 No. 1130). Physicians educated outside EU/EEA must apply for authorization or licence. A physician who has passed an examination in a foreign country is entitled to authorization if the education is recognized as being equally as good as the equivalent Norwegian examination, cf. HPA section 48a, first paragraph, litra c. The general requirements concerning fitness for the profession and age limit also apply for foreigners, as well as sufficient practical training, cf. HPA section 48a, second paragraph.

85. The HPA also contains a special provision concerning border licence, cf. section 50. Publicly employed and authorized health personnel in Sweden and Finland working along the Norwegian border can carry out their work in Norwegian municipalities without an authorization or licence.

86. Suspension and withdrawal of authorization and licence are regulated by HPA Chapter 11. The Appeals Board for Health Personnel is established as a complaint body for different forms of sanctions against health personnel, cf. HPA section 68. The board is independent, cf. section 69. In the event of judicial review, the courts may review 'all aspects of the case', cf. section 71 (in contrast to the regular, more limited review, *see* paragraph 36 *supra*). The Supreme Court has decided three cases concerning revokal of licence. In Rt. 2004 p. 1343 the licence was suspended due to an attempt of armed robbery, violence against the police and use of illicit drugs (dissent 3-2, *see also infra* paragraph 167 regarding *ne bis idem*). In Rt. 2007 p. 1851 the authorization was partly revoked and the physician was not allowed to have contact with children due to sexual abuse of children a long time ago (dissent 3-2). In Rt. 2010 p. 1613 a limited authorization was fully revoked. A doctor had been granted an authorization subject to considerable limitations due to events that took place while he was working as a general practitioner. At the time when the limited authorization was issued, he was employed as a local authority physician and the limitation prohibited him from having direct contact with patients. The limited authorization was revoked when he breached the prohibition.

48. Prop. 74 (2014–2015), 13.

87. There are (2019) about 33,400 physicians in Norway, of which about 28,500 are active and under 70 years of age. Out of these, it is about 50% of each gender.[49] As a contrast, in 1970 it was about 5,000 physicians in Norway.

II. Medical Specialists

88. The HPA stipulates that the ministry may set conditions relating to the approval of authorized health personnel as specialists within a limited area in the field of health, cf. sections 51 and 53–54. Such conditions are given by regulation on approval of specialization of health personnel and practical training of physicians (21 December 2000 No. 1384). The ministry shall define the fields of specialization within medicine. Institutions educating physicians as specialist shall be approved by the directorate of health.

89. Until the act relating to rights and duties of medical doctors was introduced in 1980 (replacing the former act from 1927) the Norwegian association of medical doctors was responsible for the education of specialists and issued diploma and certifications. The ministry has since then been responsible for specialization of physicians, but many tasks have been delegated to the Norwegian Medical Association. The provisions regarding specialization were revised in 2015 in order to clarify the ministry's competence to give further regulations and pave the way for a revised model of specialization (law of 19 June 2015 No. 60).[50] The Directorate of Health grants authorization as a specialist.

90. Most disciplines of specialization take six and a half years. The main element of the specialization is practical training under supervision, but the education also contains theoretical elements in the form of compulsory courses. Historically, the Norwegian Medical Association has provided most of the courses. The Directorate of Health has now taken over this responsibility and has developed a new model for the specialization. Regulation of 8 December 2016 No. 1482 concerns specialist education and specialist approval for physicians and dentists (Regulation on Specialization).

The new Regulation on Specialization contains important changes in the specialization structure and will seek to modernize the specialization and provide an individual educational pathway for each physician in specialization. The new specialization structure consists of three parts with related learning goals and activities. Part 1 (LIS1) replaces the current residency and applies to all physicians in specialization. The physician in specialization must complete twelve months of practice in health trust and six months in health and care services. Part 2 (LIS2) consists of common learning goals for the prior specialists in surgery and internal medicine,

49. *See* https://www.legeforeningen.no/om-oss/legestatistikk/english/ (retrieved 10 Jul 2022). This overview also contains figures from the Nordic Countries. 'Active' physician is defines at being 'and/or under age of retirement, and living/working in the country'.

50. Prop. 81 L (2014–2015) *Endringer i helsepersonelloven og helsetilsynsloven (spesialistutdanningen m.m.)* (Amendment to the Health Personnel Act and Health Supervision Act (specialist training, etc.)).

and Part 3 (LIS3) is unique for each specialization. The learning goals are stated in the Regulation on Specialization. They define what the physician should understand and be able to perform after having completed the learning process, and the physician in specialization will be assessed according to the achieved learning goals. The regional education centres at the regional hospitals will be responsible for developing and carrying out the learning activities.

91. According to the same principles as fore general education, physicians with specialization from another country can apply for recognition. Directive 2005/36/EC is applicable for physicians with a specialization from an EU or EEA Member State or Switzerland.

92. There are (2021) about 24,500 approved specialists in Norway under the age of 80 years.[51] The largest discipline of speciality is family medicine/general practice (500), followed by internal medicine (2,300) and psychiatry (1,950). In most fields the approval as specialist is valid as long as the physician has authorization or licence, but recertification is needed every fifth year for specialists in general practice.

---

51. *See supra* n. 53.

Chapter 2. The Practice of Medicine

§1. The General Requirement of Professional Conduct

93. According to the HPA physicians shall conduct their work in accordance with 'the requirements to professional responsibility and diligent care that can be expected based on their qualifications, the nature of their work and the situation in general', cf. HPA section 4. This norm of responsible conduct targets the individual physician, while similar provisions in other statutes require responsible conduct on an institutional level, cf. Specialized Health Services Act section 2-2 and Health and Care Services Act section 4-1. According to HPA section 16 facilities providing healthcare shall be organized in such a way that health personnel are able to comply with their statutory duties, which include the diligent care obligation in section 4.

94. All healthcare should as a starting point be given according to the best interest of the patient. Information, consent and participation are core elements, but all these are anchored in specific provisions and will not be elaborated here. The obligation of responsible conduct in section 4 was built on similar provisions in earlier legislation. The norm has indeed features of tort law. The elements in the assessment will to a large degree be the same within health law and tort law, although the threshold for judging a conduct for irresponsible will not necessarily be the same. Regarding criminal liability, a higher threshold is explicitly stated in the legislation. Punishment requires that health personnel have acted 'intentionally or by gross negligence', cf. HPA section 67 (*see* paragraphs 157 ff. *infra*).

95. The responsible conduct rule in HPA section 4 is a legal guideline, which is under constant development and influenced by the society's expectation to a physician. A starting point for the assessment will often by a risk analysis. As higher the risk is for severe injuries, as stricter is the requirement for a careful behaviour. The responsible conduct rule is a minimum standard, which does not oblige the physician to use all available resources, which in turn could lead to unnecessary use of resources. The wording of section 4 makes a reference to the 'situation in general'. The time dimension will often be of essence. In some situation the physician will have to act out of urgency, without the possibility to consult colleagues or other sources. Another element in the assessment of the 'situation in general' will be the available accessibility of equipment, which differs from a small hospital in a remote area to hospitals in major cities.

96. The responsible conduct rule in HPA section 4 includes an obligation for the physician to keep updated with recent developments. This requirement is according to the preparatory work especially firm for specialists.[52] The ministry also emphasized a stricter threshold for professional responsibility when the treatment is experimental or includes use of untraditional methods. In such cases, the patient

52. Ot.prp. No. 13 (1998–1999) *Om lov om helsepersonell m v (helsepersonelloven) (Regarding Act Relating to Health Personnel (The Health Personnel Act)),* 38.

must be given sufficient information in order to understand the consequences of the consent. A closer scrutiny of the justifiability of the interference is also required.

97. Although the standard covers all types of health personnel the assessment must be differentiated. The wording mentions 'qualifications' which includes basic education, specialization and practical training. The expectations of diligent care performance of a patient with heart failure will be higher for a physician than for a nurse, and higher for a specialized heart physician than for a general practitioner. The system of authorization and licensing, as well as additional specialization is a certification of the general competence of the physician. The diligent care standard is targeting the individual situation, and the physician must make sure that he or she has the necessary skills to conduct the treatment, or if it is required to call in additional expertise. Additional expertise could either be physicians with other skills or other professions. The obligation to refer patients to others, if necessary and possible, is stipulated in HPA section 4, second paragraph. This provision also emphasizes that if the patient's need so indicate, the healthcare shall be performed through cooperation and interaction with other qualified personnel.

98. In the preparatory work the ministry discusses the allocation of responsibility between different professionals and between the professionals and their employer. The owner can freely select the organization of their entity as they find useful, as long as this is conducted in a responsible way. The professional responsibility rule in HPA section is in this respect a safeguard from being instructed by others to act in an irresponsible manner.

99. Section 4, third paragraph is directly addressing the physician and the dentist. These two medical professionals shall in matters concerning respectively medicine or dentistry 'make decisions'. In questions regarding medical diagnostic and treatment, the physician will be responsible and nurses and others will have to act according to the physician's instructions. However, neither nurses nor physicians are obliged to follow instructions that are unlawful or being below the professional standard of diligent care.

100. Health personnel are autonomous when they carry out their professional duties, and cannot be instructed by employers or others. However, the provision in section 4, third paragraph giving the physician exclusive right to decide in medical issues is limited to situations of examination or treatment. In organizational matters, other health professionals may be in charge. For example, a birth unit can be led by a midwife.

101. The general requirement of professional conduct is in practice of an important legal norm. It is a legal standard, thus being rather flexible. It also leaves the profession as such with discretion, since the assessment of what is responsible conduct will depend upon the standards within the profession. One can therefore ask whether the norm will play a limited role, since actor and reviewer belong to the same group, where loyalty to the profession comes at stake. This topic raises a lot of questions that cannot be analysed in full depth here,[53] but some reflections may be of interest. First, it seems to have been a development. In early case law it was difficult for the patient to successfully claim compensation, while in more recent cases the Supreme Court have been more intense in their scrutiny of conduct by health personnel, although one should be careful upon drawing decisive conclusion from a limited material (*see also* paragraphs 146 ff.).[54] Second, the norm has to some extent moved out of the courts and into different forms of administrative bodies, like the entities under the Norwegian system of compensation to patients and the Norwegian Board of Health Supervision. Especially the latter seems rather eager to use the requirement to professional responsibility and diligent care as a legal anchor for their assessments, even if more specific provisions could have served the same purpose. A possible explanation could be that the professional responsibility and diligent care standard is partly internal since referring to the opinion by the profession itself. The critique is therefore not only external but is legitimized by being shared by the peers of the physician being subject of control.

§2. Use of Assistants

102. Health personnel's use of assistants is closely connected to the general requirement of responsible conduct, and as mentioned earlier, some questions regarding cooperation are regulated by HPA section 4. The general provision for use of assistants is found in HPA section 5. According to this provision health personnel may in their work assign certain tasks to other personnel if it is considered safe to do so based on the nature of the assigned task, the qualification of the assigned personnel and the guidance being provided. This possibility to assigns tasks to assistants is directed towards the individual health personnel, and the overall consideration is patients' safety. The assigned helper may both be health personnel with authorization and others, but the professional background of the assistant will be decisive for which task the helper can carry out. An assignment according to HPA section 5 is personal and cannot be passed on to others. The assistant will be under instruction from the health professional making the assignment, and in many situations subsequently evaluations will be recommendable. While HPA section 5 regulates the relationship between the responsible health personnel and their assistants, any healthcare provider has a general obligation to organize the entity in order to perform responsible conduct on an institutional level, cf. the Specialized Health Care Act section 2-2 and the Health and Care Services Act section 4-1. This obligation will contain divisions of tasks between different groups of health personnel.

103. According to HPA section 5, second paragraph pupils and students shall as a rule only be assigned tasks based on their need for training. This provision restricts the possibility of using students as a part of the ordinary work force. Students within medicine can apply for a licence when being in their last part of medical school.

53. Aslak Syse, Reidun Førde & Geir Sverre Braut, *Medisinske feil (Medical Wrongs)* (Gyldendal 2000).

54. Asbjørn Kjønstad, *Helserett (Health Law)* 101 (2d ed., Gyldendal 2007).

They will then be able to practice, but only under supervision of an authorized physician and with several restrictions (e.g., the competence to claim reimbursement from the National Insurance Scheme and to issue prescriptions).

§3. Emergency Healthcare

104. According to HPA section 7 physicians – as well as other health personnel – shall 'immediately' provide the healthcare they are capable of when it must be assumed that the healthcare is of vital importance (emergency healthcare). The duty to provide care – being treatment or to alleviate – must be seen in light of with the second paragraph. This part of the provision states than when in doubt as to whether the healthcare is of vital importance, health personnel shall perform the necessary examinations. Read in conjunction with the provision therefore contains two elements: examination – and if necessary – healthcare. In the following the reference is to both these elements as 'emergency healthcare'. The aim of the provision is to mark that protection of life is the core task of health services.

105. The obligation to provide emergency healthcare is limited by the provisions laid down in the PRA. HPA section 7 makes an explicit reference to PRA section 4-9 (for a more detailed presentation of PRA section 4-9, *see* paragraphs 218 ff. *infra*). According to the latter provision a patient is entitled, due to serious conviction, to refuse to receive blood or blood products and to refuse to break off an ongoing hunger strike. The provision also entitles a dying patient to object to life-prolonging treatment. HPA section 7, first paragraph, states clearly that – except for the limitations laid down in PRA section 4-9 – emergency healthcare is to be given even if the patient is incapable of granting his consent, and even if the patient objects to the treatment. The latter part of the provision is an explicit legal foundation for coercive measures (*see also* paragraph 212 *infra*). However, admission to a locked psychiatric ward requires that the conditions according to the Mental Health Care Act are fulfilled.

106. The starting point for the assessment of whether to provide emergency treatment is the severity of the patients' health condition. If there is a risk of loss of life or severe deterioration of the health condition, then physicians may be entitled to intervene, especially if the risk is high. Another element is when the negative consequence may occur, and the term emergency indicates that the situation must be acute. The duty to provide emergency healthcare is limited to the acute phase, and when this is passed healthcare can only be provided based on the ordinary conditions (normally informed consent).

107. The assessment must also include an evaluation of the probable effect of the intervention, and there should be a reluctance to intervene if it is doubtful whether the treatment will hurdle loss of life or basic functions. Possible side effects of the interventions must also be included in the assessment. In the preparatory work the ministry emphasizes that emergency healthcare even can be provided when the patients represents a threat to other persons.[55]

108. If the patient is able to make an informed consent, the starting point is the patients' autonomy. Even though the provision entitles the physician to use coercive measures, there is a certain threshold for overruling the wishes of the patient. If the patient is unconscious, the physician must evaluate whether the intervention would be in conformity with the presumed consent of the patient. In case of coercive elements there is a great variety between direct use of physical force and different forms of verbal persuasions. In such situations the ability of the patient to assess the situation will also be of importance. If a patient with a substance intoxication is admitted to an emergency ward and does not give a verbal consent to treatment in form of antidote, but does not resist by other means, such emergency treatment will be within the borders of the provision.

109. The obligation to provide emergency healthcare is a personal duty for health personnel. It will therefore apply both in the work situation as well as in spare time when a physician observes a person in need of immediate treatment in a life-threatening situation. The preparatory work emphasizes that the right to intervene and the obligation to intervene should be assessed on the same basis.[56] However, there should be some room for leeway in these two situations, especially since the provision also open up for coercive measures.

110. The duty to provide emergency healthcare is vested to all groups of health personnel. Nevertheless, the obligation does not have the same content for all groups of health personnel, and the wording limits the responsibility to 'provide the healthcare that they are capable of'. Many forms of treatment require professional skills and can therefore only be carried out by personnel with the necessary educational and practical background. HPA section 7, third paragraph is expresses a part of this division of competence. The duty to provide emergency healthcare does not apply to the extent that other qualified health personnel undertakes the responsibility to provide healthcare. In the setting of a hospital many of the emergency decisions will therefore be vested to physicians with their educational and practical background, especially if the treatment contains coercive measures.

111. It should be emphasized that HPA section 7 does not contain any procedural requirements. The competence to carry out emergency treatment can therefore be made by the individual physician, without consulting a colleague. However, if there is time for consultations and the interference is especially intrusive (high risk for the patient and/or the use of force), the requirements to professional responsibility and diligent care in HPA section 4 may warrant such a consultation. In any way the obligation to keep patients' records apply (cf. HPA Chapter 8) and the physician may be obliged to document the assessment that has been made.

---

55. Ot.prp. No. 13 (1998–1999) *Om lov om helsepersonell m v (helsepersonelloven) (Regarding Act Relating to Health Personnel (The Health Personnel Act))*, 219.
56. Ot.prp. No. 13 (1998–1999), 53.

§4. Use of Resources: Marketing

112. According to HPA section 6, health personnel shall ensure that the health-care does not mean unnecessary loss of time or unnecessary expenses to patients, health institutions, the National Insurance Scheme or others. The provision is built on previous regulations in the acts on the rights and duties of medical doctors and dentists. However, it emphasizes that this obligation also applies to health institutions and not only patients and the National Insurance Scheme.

113. The duty to reasonable use of resources applies organization of the services, including prioritization, as well as examination, diagnostics treatment and follow-up.[57] It is implied in the term 'unnecessary' that the duty to reasonable use of resources must be in conformity with the obligation of professional responsibility and diligent care, cf. HPA section 4.

114. According to HPA section 13, first paragraph, marketing of health services shall be 'responsible, factual and sober'. The same requirements apply to marketing of facilities providing healthcare, cf. section 13, second paragraph.

§5. Duty of Abstinence

115. Health personnel may not consume alcohol or other intoxicating substances during working hours, cf. HPA section 8, first paragraph. This duty of abstinence can be deducted from the norm of professional responsibility and diligent care, but is explicitly regulated to protect patient safety.

116. The provision states that medical products that are necessary due to illness are not considered to be intoxicating substances pursuant to the first paragraph. Health personnel using such products are according to the wording of the provision under an obligation as soon as possible to notify their employer thereof. Such notification by health personnel should preferably be given prior to giving treatment to the patient.

117. HPA section 8, third paragraph was amended by law of 4 May 2012 No. 23. The aim of the amendment was to clarify the duty of abstinence, and it also revised the competence for the ministry to provide further rules by regulation. According to regulation of 4 May 2012 No. 400 section 1, second paragraph, health personnel shall not consume alcohol or other intoxicating substances in the last eight hours prior to the start of their working shift. According to the regulation section 3, health personnel must not during any part of the working hours have a higher concentration of intoxicating substances in their blood than equal to 0.2 0/00 alcohol. This limit corresponds to the threshold used for driving vehicles, cf. the Traffic Act section 31.

---

57. Ot.prp. No. 13 (1998–1999) *Om lov om helsepersonell m v (helsepersonelloven) (Regarding Act Relating to Health Personnel (The Health Personnel Act)),* 219.

118. If there is a reason to believe that health personnel have violated the duty of abstinence, the employer or the county governor can impose health personnel to give a breath test, blood sample or similar examination, cf. the regulation section 2, cf. also HPA section 12. If health personnel resist or in any other way avoid testing, the employer or the county governor can require the assistance of the police, cf. the regulation section 2, second paragraph.

§6. Ban Relating to the Receiving of Gifts while Acting in a Professional Duty

119. Health personnel may not on 'on behalf of themselves or on behalf of others accept gifts, commission, service or other benefits that are suitable to affect the services by health personnel unduly', cf. HPA section 9, first paragraph. The ban is targeting economic profit, as well as other kinds of remunerations. In the preparatory work the ministry addresses specifically payment to physicians in connection to travels paid by the pharmaceutical industry.[58] Reimbursement of travel expenses and accommodation to a conference that has marketing or public relation as a main purpose may be targeted by the ban. However, the provision will not usually cover international congresses or research meetings that give health personnel a professional outcome, even if companies from the pharmaceutical industry act as sponsors. The ban is targeting both health personnel themselves as well as on 'behalf of others'. A practical example is gifts, etc. being beneficial to relatives of health personnel, typically family accompanying health personnel on congresses, etc.

120. When assessing whether the benefit is considered to be 'unduly' it will be of importance if the health personnel's employer is informed about the benefit, and has given their approval. The ministry emphasizes the need of transparency in order to have an ongoing general discussion about the connections between health personnel and commercial actors.

121. HPA section 9, second paragraph states that health personnel may furthermore 'not accept gifts, commission services or other benefits from patients', unless the gift, etc. is of 'insignificant value'. By 'insignificant value' the ministry in the preparatory work suggested a limit of NOK 1,000 (approx. EUR 100) in 1998 value.[59] However, this threshold only provides guidance. In relation to extraordinary occasions a gift may be of higher value without being 'unduly'. In other situations, a lower amount may be banned, and the conditions of the patients may be taken into consideration. The ministry uses as an example as an unduly gift that health personnel receives a gift from a patient suffering for dementia worth NOK 800 (approx. EUR 80).

58. Ot.prp. No. 13 (1998–1999) *Om lov om helsepersonell m v (helsepersonelloven) (Regarding Act Relating to Health Personnel (The Health Personnel Act))*, 221.
59. Ot.prp. No. 13 (1998–1999), 221.

122. When it comes to pharmaceutical products the ban in HPA section 8 must be read in conjunctions with the regulation on pharmaceutical products (18 December 2009 No. 1839). According to this regulation marketing to health personnel must not include any kind of benefits of economic value, cf. section 13-10. However, the provision exempts goods of insignificant value that are given in connection to the health personnel's professional activity. Expenses in relation to commercial activities shall always be kept at a reasonable level and be closely connected to the main purpose of the meeting.

§7. Requisition of Medicinal Products for Which a Prescription Is Required

123. According to HPA section 11 physicians and dentists have a statutory right to make a requisition. Other groups of health personnel holding an authorization or licence may be granted a limited right of requisition by regulations issued by the Ministry. Such a limited right is for example granted to midwives and public health nurses. If they have sufficient education beyond qualification they can prescribe contraceptives to females between 16 and 19 years old in the municipal school health service.

124. Requisition of medicinal products is a fundamental part of health services, and is closely connected to the system of prescriptions. The Medicines Act gives regulations on marketing and sales of medicinal products, and more detailed provisions are given by regulation on requisition and distribution of medicinal products from pharmacies (27 April 1998 No. 455).[60] Many medicinal products are only legally accessible by prescription and only physicians with authorization have a general right to make a requisition and provide the patient with a prescription.

125. Before a medicinal product is granted marketing licence the Norwegian Medicines Agency shall decide if the medicinal product only shall be accessible if prescribed, cf. regulation relating to medicinal products (18 December 2009 No. 1839, which will be replaced by regulation of 7 June 2022 No. 977 when this enters into force 1 January 2023) section 7-1. At the same time the Norwegian Medicines Agency shall place the product into prescription group A-C. Reception group A is typically for products containing narcotic substances or that can be addictive, cf. section 7-3.

§8. Examinations in Connection with a Criminal Offence

126. The obligation of physicians (and other groups of health personnel) to carry out tests and examinations in connection with criminal offences is a distinct form of duty. It is not rooted in the need of the patient, but is given by public desires. The

60. *See also* the homepage of the Norwegian Medicines Agency https://legemiddelverket.no/English (accessed 10 Jul. 2022).

provision has therefore been disputed. When health personnel are conducting their duties according to section 12 they are not under an obligation of confidentiality. The result of the tests and examinations can therefore be communicated to the authorities.

127. According to section 12, first paragraph a physician, nurse or medical laboratory technologist shall, upon request form the police, take a blood test or perform a similar examination of persons suspected of a criminal offence under the influence of alcohol or other intoxicating or narcotic substance when this is in accordance with statutory law and may be performed without danger. The consent of the person concerned is not a requirement for carrying out such a test. The provision is especially practical for cases of driving vehicles under the influence of alcohol or other intoxicating substances, which in Norway is rather heavy penalized compared with other countries (normally a fine equivalent to the offenders 1.5 monthly salary before taxes, combined with imprisonment, which may be conditional). The introduction of breath analyses has reduced the need of blood samples in cases concerning alcohol, but other substances still require blood samples.

128. According to section 12, second paragraph a physician shall upon request from the prosecuting authority perform a physical examination of suspects in a criminal case when such an examination has been decided pursuant to the Criminal Procedure Code section Such an examination can only be carried out if decided by the prosecuting authority, and differs in this respect from HPA section 12, first paragraph where a request from the police is sufficient. The consent of the patient is not a requirement for carrying out such an examination. The provision is authorizing bodily investigations, i.e., in the ear or in rectum. Social inquiry and forensic psychiatric observation within the criminal procedure is regulated by the Criminal Procedure Act Chapter 13. Besides the duties elaborated here, section 12 also contains provisions on tests and examination relating to execution of sentences, cf. section 12, second paragraph, second sentence and section 12, third paragraph.

129. Section 12, fourth paragraph stipulates the exceptions from the duty to carry out tests and examinations permitted by the previous paragraphs. According to litra a) health personnel are not obliged to carry out tests or examinations if they are closely related to the person concerned. According to litra b) health personnel are exempted to perform examinations on persons they are providing medical treatment for. The provision is given to protect an established relationship between the health personnel and a patient. The extension of this exemption was decided by the Supreme Court in Rt. 2005 p. 1329. A person was brought to hospital after a car accident, where he was severely injured together with a passenger. Another passenger died. The said patient was suspected of having driven the car under the influence of alcohol. The police requested a blood sample according to section 12, first paragraph. By unclear reasons such a test was performed more than eighteen hours after the accident and was therefore useless for the purposes. The public prosecutor then requested the hospital to hand over blood samples taken as part of the ordinary medical treatment shortly after the arrival to the hospital. The hospital denied submitting the tests referring to their medical confidentiality. The Supreme Court held by 4-1 votes that section 12, first paragraph had to be interpreted according to the strict wording of the provision. The duty to assist the police with testing is transposing the ordinary tasks of health personnel. It could therefore not be taken into account that the missing test represented an accidental advantage of the suspect.

§9. Duty Rota

130. According to HPA section 14 the ministry may determine that health personnel shall participate in a duty rota at their place of residence or their place of work. The aim of the provision is to secure the public access to emergency healthcare. There is an implied limitation that voluntarily measures in forms of agreements have to be unsuccessful before duty rota can be introduced. Normally, agreements are made on a voluntary basis between the organizations of health personnel and the employers. The obligation to participate in a duty rota is limited to the health personnel's place of residence or their place of work.

131. Norway is a scarcely populated country and rural areas have faced difficulties with attracting health personnel, especially in the northern part. For dentists, a previous system of compulsory civil service was established by law. The system was challenged both by an individual dentist (Rt. 1961 p. 1350) and by the Association of Norwegian Dentists (Rt. 1966 p. 476), claiming it was unconstitutional and violated the European Convention on Human Rights (ECHR). In both cases the Supreme Court held that the challenged rules were lawful. The majority of the European Commission of Human Rights concluded that the Norwegian system was not a violation of Article 4 and the prohibition of 'forced or compulsory labour'.[61] A similar system of compulsory civil service was never introduced for physicians. However, similar effects have been achieved by the former system of practical training ('turnus'), *see supra* paragraph 70.

§10. Requirements to Medical Reports, Medical Certification, Etc.

132. Medical reports play a significant role in many situations, both in the public and private sector. According to HPA section 15, anyone who issues a medical certification, a medical report or similar documents shall be careful, precise and objective. The provision applies both when HPA as an expert (cf. section 27) and when HPA as part of an ongoing patient relationship. HPA section 15 also requires that a medical report shall be correct, and contain only such information that is necessary for the intended purpose. These requirements have both a bearing to the trustworthy of the document (being correct) and the integrity of the patient (only disclosing information necessary for the purpose). If the report is submitted upon a request from the patient, the patient must consent to the use of medical information.

61. *I. v. Norway*, Appl. No. 1468/62, decision 17 Dec. 1963.

133. Section 15, first paragraph was amended in 2008, partly due to some debated cases concerning medical reports, cf. act 9 May 2009 No. 34. In the preparatory work, the ministry stated that many of the amendments where technical adjustments of the existing wording.[62] Additionally, the provision was also clarified. According to HPA section 15, first paragraph, third sentence medical reports shall contain all information that the health personnel should understand is of importance for the receiver and the purpose of the report. Health personnel shall clearly indicate if the report is based only on a limited part of the relevant information available for the health personnel. These clarifications are made in order to strengthen the validity of the reports by stating what information the report should be based on. Many disputes between physicians and their patients arise when physicians are submitting medical reports (*see infra* paragraph 184 concerning cases from the medical ethics committee).

134. Another amendment was also made in 2008, at this occasion as a part of the revision of the statutory framework for insurance companies' collection, use and storage of health information. When health personnel understand that it can be of special relevance how distinctive sensitive factual circumstances are being described in a medical report to an insurance company, he or she should consult the patient, cf. HPA section 15, second paragraph. This provision is in the preparatory work considered as a derivation of the general requirement in HPA section 15, first paragraph.[63] HPA section 15, third paragraph is targeting information that can be taken as a sign of a severe illness. If such information is to be submitted to an insurance company, the patient is to be given a prior notification. The aim is to avoid that patients are being informed of severe conditions by the insurance company and not by their doctors.

135. HPA section 15, first paragraph, last sentence refers to the PAA section 6, which contains provisions on impartiality for public servants. If a health personnel has such a link to the patient that he or she would have been considered impartial when taking an administrative decision, then the health personnel is considered disqualified to issue a medical report. If a report is made despite that the issuer has such a close relationship to the patient as set forth in the PAA section 6, the report as such is not invalid. However, the violation of HPA section 15 can have an impact on administrative or the decisions taken on the basis of the report.

136. An ongoing debate in Norway has been physicians' role in sick leaves, and if they are too generous when giving sick leave certificates. The discussions must be viewed on the background that employees have full compensation when being

62. Ot.prp. No. 25 (2007–2008) *Om lov om endringer i helsepersonelloven og helseregisterloven (krav til helsepersonells attester, erklæringer o.l., administrative reaksjoner og forbud mot urettmessig tilegnelse av helseopplysninger) (Regarding Act Relating to Amendments in the Health Personnel Act and the Health Registers Act (Requirements to Health Personnels' Certifications, Report, Etc., Administrative Sanctions and Prohibition against Unjust Use of Health Information)),* 23–25.
63. Ot.prp. No. 41 (2007–2008) *Om lov om endringer i lov 16. juni 1989 nr. 69 om forsikringsavtaler m.m. (Regarding Act Relating to Amendments to Act 16 Jun. 1989 No. 69 Relating to Insurance Contracts, Etc.,)* 103.

on sick leave (the first period covered by the employer and later period by the National Insurance Scheme). The employee can make a personal declaration for shorter leaves, but in the event of sick leaves lasting several days, the employer can require a sick leave certificate from a physician (some other groups of health personnel can also issue such certificates). The requirements and procedures for documentation of a condition justifying sick leave have been revised at several occasions on order to avoid unnecessary absence from work.

Chapter 3. Illegal Practice of Medicine

137. As in other fields of the society, the starting point is that a person can take up activity in a certain field without seeking permission from the authorities. Counter wise, any person may receive treatment as he or she may prefer. These starting points are within the field of health law partly rhetoric. The Alternative Treatment Act (replacing a previous act from 1936) regulates the medical field, and gives partly health personnel an entitled right to provide medical treatment in order to protect the patients' safety. An expert committee appointed by the government made a draft of the act.[64] The act uses the term 'patient' ('pasient'), although persons receiving alternative treatment from not authorized health personnel are not entitled to rights according to the PRA.[65] The Norwegian health authorities have launched an information website about complementary and alternative medicine. It is run by Norway's National Research Centre in Complementary and Alternative Medicine (NAFKAM). Nifab.no shall provide the Norwegian population with evidence-based information about complementary and alternative medicine.[66]

138. The objective of the Alternative Treatment Act is two-folded. The act shall contribute to 'safety for the patients' who seek or receive alternative treatment and the act shall regulate the right to practice such treatment, cf. section 1. The act applies to persons 'offering or practising' alternative treatment in Norway, cf. section 2, first paragraph. Insofar as they are appropriate, the regulations regarding territorial scope issued in pursuance of HPA section 2 shall also apply to the Alternative Treatment Act. The aim is to achieve the parallel territorial scope of the two acts given their similar character. In the preparatory work, the ministry emphasizes that the act will also apply in cases where there is no direct contact between the patient and the person offering alternative treatment, i.e., advices given by telephone, email and videoconferences.[67] Ordinary religious practices will nevertheless fall outside the scope of the act, although border cases may arise.

139. According to the Alternative Treatment Act section 2, third paragraph alternative treatment is defined as 'health related treatment which is practiced outside the established health services' and which is not practised by authorized health personnel. However, the latter is elaborated when the provision continues to state that treatment practised 'within the scope of the established health services' or by authorized health personnel[68] is also covered by the term alternative treatment when the

64. NOU 1998:21 *Alternativ medisin (Alternative Medicine).*
65. Ot.prp. No. 27 (2002–2003) *Om lov om alternativ behandling ved sykdom mv. (Regarding Act Relating to Alternative Treatment of Diseases, Etc.,)* 125.
66. http://nafkam.no/en (accessed 10 Jul. 2019).
67. Ot.prp. No. 27 (2002–2003) *Om lov om alternativ behandling ved sykdom mv. (Regarding Act Relating to Alternative Treatment of Diseases, Etc.,)* 121.
68. This term covers both personnel with authorization (HPA s. 48) and with licence (HPA s. 49), cf. Ot.prp. No. 27 (2002–2003), 205.

methods used are 'essentially' used outside the established health services. The preparatory works use acupuncture as an example of a kind of alternative treatment commonly used by authorized health personnel within the ordinary health services.[69]

140. According to section 5, medical intervention or treatment which may entail a serious health hazard for patients shall only be practised by health personnel. The act does not define 'serious health hazard', but in the preparatory works the ministry emphasized that the assessment should be made on the basis of the intervention or treatment as such, and not the risk for the individual patient.[70] If the intervention as such does not represent a serious health hazard, but may do so for the individual patient due to personal conditions, the penal provision may apply.

141. The treatment of serious diseases and disorders shall only be practised by health personnel, cf. section 7, first paragraph. Diseases and disorders include both somatic and psychiatric conditions. As with section 5 the assessment on whether condition is serious shall be made on a general basis, while individual vulnerability may invoke the penal provision.[71] Non-health personnel may nevertheless administer treatment for patients in cases where the sole purpose is to alleviate or moderate symptoms or consequences of the disease or side effects of given treatment or where the purpose is to strengthen the body's immune system or its ability to heal itself, cf. section 7, second paragraph. This provision is based on a division between the disease itself and the given treatment. Health personnel are given monopoly to identify (diagnose) and treat the disease itself, while non-health personnel may provide alternative treatment targeting conditions deriving from the disease or targeting the immune system. The exception for alternative treatment is based on an assumption that this form of approach is not too risky for the patient.

142. Furthermore, alternative treatment can be given if the treatment takes place in 'cooperation with or in consultation with' the patient's physician and the patient is of age and entitled to consent to healthcare pursuant to PRA section 4-3, first and second paragraph, cf. the Alternative Treatment Act section 7, third paragraph. This exception is also based on a kind of risk assumption, but at this time made on an assessment by the physician, who either must cooperate or act in consultation with non-health personnel. Additionally, the provisions in the HPA concerning ability to consent must be fulfilled. A decision to enter alternative treatment is considered to be of such importance that the patients must have reached the age of 18 years. Alternative treatment may also be offered to other groups of patients, i.e., minors and those without the capacity to consent, but on the condition that the health service has no curative or palliative treatment to offer the patient, cf. the Alternative Treatment Act section 7, third paragraph, second sentence (with additional requirements in third sentence). Since these patients cannot consent on their own behalf, the accessibility to alternative treatment is more limited.

---

69. Ot.prp. No. 27 (2002–2003), 121–122.
70. Ot.prp. No. 27 (2002–2003), 206–207.
71. Ot.prp. No. 27 (2002–2003), 208.

143. Turning to treatment of communicable diseases that are hazardous to public health, this shall only be practised by health personnel, cf. the Alternative Treatment Act section 6. The coverage of diseases is made by a reference to the Communicable Diseases Act section 1-3. The rationale for the provision is that communicable diseases pose such a threat for both the patient and the society that health personnel must be responsible for treatment. Based on the same approach as the exceptions in section 7, non-health personnel may nevertheless administer treatment in cases where the sole purpose is to alleviate or moderate symptoms or consequences of the disease or side effects of given treatment, cf. the Alternative Treatment Act section 6, second paragraph. Non-health personnel may also here administer treatment where the purpose is to strengthen the body's immune system or it ability to heal itself.

144. When introducing the Alternative Treatment Act the ministry also established a voluntary registration scheme for health personnel and others who practice alternative treatment, cf. section 3. More detailed provisions of the register are given by regulation (11 December 2003 No. 1500). The aim of the register is to contribute to improved patient' safety and consumer rights for those seeking a registered person providing alternative treatment, cf. the regulation section 1. Additional, the register shall contribute to seriousness and sound business among those providing alternative treatment. In order to be registered the person providing alternative treatment must be member of an organization approved by the Directorate of Health. The regulation stipulated several conditions for an organization to be approved, including establishing a procedure for complaints, cf. section 3. There is a fee for entering the register and a yearly fee for continuing to be registered. The register must be deemed successful, and more than sixty organizations are approved. The register is accessible for the general public by a website. Until recently, alternative treatment was exempted from value-added tax, if the person provided treatment was registered in the register, which partly can explain that so many registered. From 1 January 2021 alternative treatment is no longer exempted from value-added tax.

145. Only persons who are registered as practitioners of alternative treatment in the register established pursuant to section 3 may use the designation 'registered' along with their professional title of alternative therapist, cf. section 8, fourth paragraph. The professional title as an alternative therapist is not as such protected. The author of this chapter could therefore start up as a 'healer' – but only being a 'registered' healer if a member of one of the three approved healer organizations – or introduce a new profession as 'lawshaman'.

146. According to the Alternative Treatment Act section 4, the provisions relating to the duty of confidentiality in HPA sections 21–25 shall correspondingly apply to non-health personnel who practice alternative treatment, insofar as the said provisions are appropriate. The application of the norms of health personnel relating to confidentiality is made in order to protect the patient. The enforcement is supported by penal sanctions according to the Alternative Treatment Act section 9, which has the same maximum penalty as HPA section 67. However, in trials before the courts, only specific professions such as physicians are exempted from the obligation to make a testimony, cf. the Criminal Procedure Code section 119 and the Civil Procedure Code section 22-5.

147. Any person who infringes the provisions of the Alternative Treatment Act are subject to punishment, either by fines or by term of imprisonment not exceeding three months, cf. section 9, first paragraph. Punishment requires that the person concerned has 'wilfully or through gross negligence' infringed the provisions of the act. Both the required level of *mens rea* and maximum penalty are formulated to be in conformity with the penal provisions in HPA section 67.[72]

148. Non-health personnel who 'by medical intervention or treatment' wilfully or by negligence[73] place a person's life or health in serious danger, either by the treatment itself or because the patient as a result of the treatment omits to seek help, may also be punished, cf. section 9, second paragraph. This provision applies only to 'non-health personnel' since health personnel are under the obligation of professional conduct according to HPA. Furthermore, the provision is targeting acts or omissions which are not covered by the other provisions in the Alternative Treatment Act. In the preparatory works, the ministry uses as an example a person providing alternative treatment that according to a common assessment would not entail a serious health hazard for the patient, but where particular elements in the carrying out of the treatment or by a specific patient is leading to serious consequences.[74] It should be noted that the required level of *mens rea* is lowered compared to section 9, first paragraph.

149. In particularly aggravating circumstances, a term of imprisonment not exceeding two years may be imposed, cf. section 9, third paragraph. Whether particularly aggravating circumstances is considered to exist, depends on an overall assessment, where some guidelines are formulated in the provision, cf. section 9, third paragraph, second sentence.

150. Section 9, fourth paragraph contains a rather unusual provision and addresses the assessment of *mens rea*. The fact that the person in question 'did not understand or should have understood' the danger or the nature of the disease does not exempt the person from punishment. In the preparatory works the ministry justifies the provision by stating that it should not be unpunished to provide treatment and use an excuse that one did not understand the risk or the nature of the disease.[75] The ministry uses as an example that the person providing alternative treatment out of lack of professional knowledge did not understand or should have understood the risk of the treatment.

---

72. Ot.prp. No. 27 (2002–2003), 212.
73. The unofficial translation is here misleading and using the term 'gross negligence'.
74. Ot.prp. No. 27 (2002–2003), 212.
75. Ot.prp. No. 27 (2002–2003), 212.

151. The only case relating to the Alternative Treatment Act before the Supreme Court was concerning the procedural requirements of public prosecution, cf. Rt. 2007 p. 382. The core of the matter was that the indictment was referring to section 9, second paragraph. In such cases the decision of public prosecution is vested to the district attorney and not the police. Rt. 2006 p. 535 is a case prior to the Alternative Treatment, concerning a healer convicted for violation of the Penal Code for negligent infliction of considerable harm to body or health (former Penal Code section 238, cf. current Penal Code Section 280). The healer had prescribed a patient with calcium tablets for arm problems. The high intake of calcium led to cardiac arrest and subsequent brain damages. The Supreme Court held that, normally, such acts would lead to five months of imprisonment, but reduced the punishment to sixty days of imprisonment due to the lengthy proceeding (more than three years). There are reported criminal cases concerning the Alternative Treatment Act. An illustrative case is LF-2015-38129 (Frostating High Court 28 September 2015). A 'healer' offering services to a patient with metastatic cancer aiming to cure the disease was convicted to sixty days imprisonment (on probation). The patient abstained from chemotherapy in order to prioritize the alternative treatment. Even though the patient had consented to the alternative treatment, the 'healer' had mislead the patient and had her to refrain medical treatment that could alleviated her pains and prolonged her life. When making the sentence conditional the high court paid particular attention to the long duration of the criminal procedure.

Chapter 4. Control over the Practice of Medicine

§1. Professional Liability

I. Civil Liability

152. There are reported cases on civil liability for physicians from the beginning of the twentieth century. One early example before the Supreme Court is the case reported in Rt. 1914 p. 913. After casting of a broken leg, the wound expanded and was infected leading to an amputation. The patient claimed that the physician had acted of negligence. As in other fields, the legal foundation of a compensation claim is the ordinary norm of culpability within civil law, which in Norway is developed by the courts. The Supreme Court found that the physician had acted with sufficient care and the claim was unsuccessful.

153. Claims from patients after medical treatment came regularly before the courts during the last century, but in most cases the patients' claim was unsuccessful.[76] The first case before the Supreme Court awarding compensation to the patient was Rt. 1951 p. 950. This case was also concerning a broken leg in a cast. Based on the expert assessments the Supreme Court held that the physician had not followed up the patient to a sufficient degree, even though hospital facilities were available nearby. The patient's claim was also successful in Rt. 1960 p. 841. After being vaccinated against smallpox (variola), which was compulsory for those signing on ship going overseas, the patient was infected with meningitis. The Supreme Court held that the vaccination was given in the interest of the public and was part of a mandatory scheme. It was therefore reasonable that the society also took the financial burden for these kinds of side effects. Although the last two cases indicate that patients' could be entitled to compensation, in most instances the Supreme Court held the physicians had acted with sufficient care. It was an ongoing discussion whether physicians where subject to a milder diligent standard than other professions.

154. The unclear legal landscape was considered to be inexpedient. Physicians and hospitals risked a loss of prestige if affirming responsibility and it was a financial burden for the patients to pursue their claims before the court. After Sweden introduced a compensation scheme for patients in 1975, voices suggested that a similar system should be established also in Norway. A draft was launched in 1977 by the interest organization of Norwegian municipalities and several insurance companies, but the case was not prioritized by the ministry. In 1987, the government introduced a temporary system of compensation after patient injuries. It was based on an agreement between the state and the county municipality, which at that time was responsible for the hospitals. The temporary scheme was not made in the form of legislation. It could therefore in principle be abolished by a decision by the government, although such an approach was very unlikely. The temporary scheme was

---

76. For an overview of the development, *see* Aslak Syse, Reidun Førde & Asbjørn Kjønstad, *Medisinske feil (Medical Faults)* (Gyldendal 2000).

later supplemented with similar provisions for psychiatric hospitals and outpatient clinics and for municipal medical services.

155. The same year as the temporary scheme was introduced the government appointed an expert committee to prepare a draft for a permanent act on compensation for patient injuries. The committee delivered their report in 1992.[77] The ministry made their proposition for the parliament in 1998.[78] Due to the major health law reform (*see supra* paragraph 54), the ministry had to make some adjustments, and a new proposition was submitted the next year.[79] The Patient's Injury Act came into force on 1 January 2003. More detailed provisions are given in regulation of 20 December 2002 No. 1625.

156. The Patient Compensation Act established the Norwegian system of compensation to patients (*Norsk Pasientskaderstatning*), headed by a board, which decides compensations claims from patients, cf. section 9.[80] This decision can be appealed by the patient to the patients' injury compensation board, cf. section 15. It consists of five permanent members. The leader is a lawyer and two members shall be medical experts. At least one of the members shall represent the patients as a group. Both the Norwegian system of compensation to patients and the patients' injury compensation board are independent administrative bodies which cannot be instructed by the ministry when it comes to interpretation of the law, administrative discretion and assessment of individual cases, cf. regulation of 20 December 2002 No. 1625 section 2. A decision by the Patients' Injury Compensation Board can be challenged for the courts by the patient claiming compensation.[81]

157. The state, the regional health enterprises and the municipalities are obliged to contribute to the patients' injury compensation scheme in order to cover the damages paid to the patients and covering the administrative costs, cf. section 7. Those offering health and care services outside the public sector are also obliged to make a contribution, cf. section 8. The ministry can by regulations stipulate that providers could or should take out an insurance to cover the responsibilities according to the act, cf. section 8a.

158. The Patient's Injury Act covers injuries caused in institutions under specialized health services and the municipal health and care services, during ambulance transport and by health personnel providing health services according to public authorization or licence, cf. section 1. The system also covers injuries after

77. NOU 1992:6 *Erstatning ved pasientskader (Compensation after Patient Injuries).*
78. Ot.prp. No. 31 (1998–1999) *Om lov om erstatning ved pasientskader (pasientskadeloven) (Regarding Act Relating to Patient Injuries (Patient's Compensation Act)).*
79. Ot.prp. No. 55 (1999–2000) *Om lov om erstatning ved pasientskader (pasientskadeloven) (Regarding Act Relating to Patient Injuries (Patient's Compensation Act).*
80. For an overview in English of the Norwegian Compensation scheme, *see* https://www.npe.no/en/ (accessed 10 Jul. 2022).
81. For an overview of the Scandinavian model compared with the US system, *see* Barry Furrow and Karl Harald Søvig, Medical Liability: Comparing Compensation Systems, in *The Oxford Handbook of Comparative Health Law* (eds. Tamara Hervey and David Orentlicher), 2021, 559–601.

health services provided abroad in cases of breach of the individual fixed time limit for treatment or where no adequate medical services are available within the realm, cf. section 19 with further references to PRA section 2-1b, fourth and fifth paragraphs.

159. The patient, and others having a loss due to patient injuries, are entitled to compensation when the injury is caused by (section 2, first paragraph):

(a) failures during health services, even though no individual can be blamed;
(b) technical failures of device, instrument or other equipment used during provision of health services;
(c) contamination or infection, when this is not mainly caused by the patients' condition of disease;
(d) vaccination; or
(e) circumstances warranting liability for health and care services or health personnel according to established compensation rules.

160. It should be taken into consideration whether the expectations that the patient reasonably can have to the activity or to the services have been disregarded, cf. section 2, second paragraph. The provision continues to state that insufficient resources shall not lead to liability if the allocation of resources has been acceptable and the service is commonly holding a reasonable standard. Even though there is no foundation for liability according to section 2, first and second paragraph, compensation can be awarded if a patient injury has occurred which is especially severe or unexpected, and that cannot be considered as an outcome of a risk that the patient must bear, cf. section 2, third paragraph. In this assessment it shall according to the provision be taken into consideration if the patient has been given sufficient information in beforehand.

161. Civil lawsuits from patients are common, and some of these reach the Supreme Court. Some cases from recent years will be presented here in order to illustrate some of the contemporary issues in Norwegian Health Law. In Rt. 2013 p. 1689, a mother claimed compensation after giving birth to a child with Downs's syndrome. The couple had already three children, of them was a pair of twins with special needs. Based on their care responsibilities, the woman had decided to terminate the pregnancy if the forthcoming child was expected to have disabilities. The woman was referred to the hospital, which did not carry out an amniocentesis. After giving birth, the mother was diagnosed with generalized anxiety disorder with recurrent depression that was caused by the burden of raising a child with disabilities. It was acknowledged to be a failure in the treatment, but the claim for compensation was rejected since the birth of a child with Downs's syndrome was considered to fall outside the scope of tort law. An important legal background for this care was the previous judgment in Rt. 1999 p. 203. A unanimous Supreme Court then held that expenses for raising a child after failed sterilization was not considered as an injury and was outside the scope of tort law. This judgment served as a precedent, but the Supreme Court was in Rt. 2013 p. 1689 divided in their approach. The majority (three judges) held that awarding the mother with compensation would undermine the principles established in the sterilization judgment. Additionally, providing compensation would cause challenges where to draw the demarcation line as well as evidential issues. The minority (two judges) emphasized the fundamental differences between expenses relating to a condition suffered by the mother and expenses relating to raising a child. In HR-2018-1056-A the patient inflicted nerve damage to his legs during hip surgery, caused by pressure against both thigh nerves. The Supreme Court held that the conditions for compensation pursuant to the Patient Injury Act section 3 that the injury must be caused by an exterior factor and that the cause of the injury must be unclear had been met. The provision is however an evidence rule and not a provision on strict liability. It does not permit exemptions from the basic condition in section 2 subsection 1a that error must be established in the provision of healthcare. Standard procedure had been followed, and it was assumed that no error had been committed. The appeal against the Court of Appeal's judgment in favour of the respondent was dismissed. In HR-2018-2080-A a 15-year-old boy had died while in hospital due to healthcare failure. The boy was admitted to hospital due to stomach pain and he was severely handicapped without language. The Supreme Court found that the boy's mother, who had found him dead, was entitled to compensation from the state under section 2 subsection 1(a) of the Patient Injury Act for the mental injury she had suffered. The parties agreed that there existed a basis for liability under the Patient Injury Act and a causal relationship between the healthcare failure and the mother's mental injury, and the Supreme Court also found that the injury was not so unforeseeable and remote as to exclude liability. The discussion was based on the so-called shock injury judgment – and the Court held that the legal status expressed in these judgments could be justified to some extent. The Court also referred to recent years' trends related to the same type of injury and to the current starting point that mental injury is equal to physical injury under tort law. Also, the case law referred to is not entirely compatible with the basic vulnerability principle in tort law. For more than years, tort law experts have questioned the Supreme Court's practice in the so-called shock injury cases. The district court's judgment, imposing liability on the state represented by the Patient Injury Compensation Board, was upheld. In HR-2020-1332-A, a patient who had been examined for heart flutter had not been informed that treatment with blood-thinning medicine to prevent a stroke was not considered necessary. According to good medical practice, he should have been consulted about this. The patient later incurred a stroke for a different reason than the heart flutter. There was an agreement that blood-thinning treatment could not have prevented the stroke, but it could have limited the extent of the injury. A unanimous Supreme Court found that the failure to inform the patient about the choice of treatment constituted a failure in the provision of healthcare, cf. Patient Injury Act section 2 subsection 1 (a). A majority of three justices found, however, that the added injury, which was not caused by the heart shutter for which the patient had been treated, was a too distant and derived consequence of the information failure for any liability to be established. A minority of two justices found that the added injury was an effect of the risk created by the failure in the provision of healthcare, and that the patient was entitled to damages. In HR-2022-1132-A, a child had sustained serious brain damage during delivery at a Norwegian hospital. The parents, who had met each other in the USA, came to Norway a couple of months before the delivery and moved back to the USA shortly after. The Supreme Court found, unlike the lower instances, that the compensation for medical and socio-medical costs had to be calculated based on the level of expenditures in the USA, and that no regard should be had to the welfare benefits the child would have received if the family had stayed in Norway. Emphasis was placed on the seriousness of the child's brain damage, the family's affiliation with the USA and strong humanitarian considerations. Given the major differences between USA and Norway when it comes to public social services, the outcome will lead to a significant higher compensation when the case is tried again at the High Court. The plaintiffs had been awarded around NOK 10 million (approx. EUR 1 Million), while the claim was around NOK 55 million (approx. EUR 5.5 millions). The differences relate to the coverage of expected expenses for care, which in Norway is to a last extent covered by public services, while in USA it must be purchased by private providers

162. Many of the claims from patients were historically dismissed by the courts due to unsatisfactory evidence. An illustrative case is Rt. 1980 p. 1299. The patient claimed compensation after an arm surgery. The hospital was not found liable, and a central part of the reasoning by the Supreme Court was the evidence situation, where only some of the possible alternatives causing the injury could be seen as a result of negligence by the health personnel during the surgery and the post-operative phase. Patient's Injury Act section 3, first paragraph addresses unsolved causal relations. If the causation of an injury of a patient cannot be established, and the injury most likely is due to outer circumstances influencing the patient during treatment, it should normally be presumed that the injury is caused by negligence or failure during provision of health services. The Patient's Injury Act section 3, second paragraph regulates compensation as a consequence of injuries after recommended or compulsory vaccinations according to the Communicable Diseases Act. The patient is entitled to compensation according to the Patient's Injury Act section 2, first paragraph litra d) unless the responsible body establishes beyond reasonable doubt (*godtgjør*) that one or several other causes are more likely. In Rt. 2015 p. 1246, a 12 year-old boy had been diagnosed with multiple sclerosis just a couple of months after being vaccinated for the second time (the ordinary MMR vaccine programme provided to all children). After a review of the expert reports the Supreme Court came to the conclusion that it was a practical possibility that the vaccine could cause the disease. The boy would not in foreseeable future have developed multiple sclerosis without the vaccination. Since no other cause was more likely than the vaccination, the Supreme Court held the state liable.

163. If the injury falls within the scope of section 2 and the patient is entitled to compensation, the quantification of damages is made according the Compensation Act and customary tort law, cf. the Patient's Compensation Act section 4. As a general principle in Norwegian tort law the injured shall have compensated their individual economic loss.[82] The Injury Act has two provisions making an exception from this starting point. According to section 3-2, the injured person is entitled to

82. *See* Bjarte Askeland, *Basic Questions of Tort Law from a Norwegian Perspective*, in *Basic Questions of Tort Law from a Comparative Perspective* 120 (Helmut Koziol ed., Jan Sramek 2015).

damages for pain and suffering, if the injury is permanent and prominent. According to section 3-5, the injured person is entitled to satisfactory compensation if the offender has acted wilfully or with gross negligence. The Patient's Rights Act section 4 makes two exceptions from the general rules of compensation. First, satisfactory compensation is not covered by the patients' injury compensation scheme. Such damages must be directed to the offender in person. Second, the loss must exceed NOK 5,000 (approx. EUR 500). The minimum loss was debated during the preparation of the act. It was justified with reference to the cost of administering minor injuries, as well with a reference to the state of law in the other Nordic countries.[83] The amount has not been changed since the introduction of the act. Given the inflation, it plays a minor role today.

164. The Patient's Injury Act does not restrict an injured patient from seeking compensation from other than the patients' injury compensation scheme, cf. section 4, third paragraph. However, injuries that are covered by the act cannot be claimed by the state and other public entities. Claims under the Patient's Injury Act are subject to the same rules of prescriptions as other claims, cf. section 5.

165. The number of cases and expenses for damages has been increasing in recent years, while the percentage of patients being successful of their claims has been stable (around 28%). In 2018, the Norwegian system of compensation to patients received 6,553 cases and the total amount of payments just exceeded NOK 1 billion (approx. EUR 100 million).[84] The average case processing time is seven months (thirteen months including the evaluation of compensation claim). About 33% of the patients having rejected their claim by Norwegian system of compensation to patients appeal to the patients' injury compensation board. The patients' injury compensation board received last year (2021) 1,097 cases.[85] The average case processing time is twenty-two months. In 2021, the patients' injury compensation board received 188 writs of summons.

II. Criminal Liability

166. According to section 96 of the Constitution, no one can be convicted unless prescribed by law. General provisions on criminal liability are laid down in the Penal Code. The Penal Code was replaced in 2005, but the new act first came into force on 1 October 2015. Many provisions are a linguistic overhaul of the earlier legislation, and decisions under the former act (Penal Code 1902) is therefore still of relevance. In addition to the rules in the Penal Code, penal provisions are found in sectorial regulations. The latter will be presented first. According to HPA section 67, anyone who 'intentionally or by gross negligence' contravenes the 'provisions

83. Ot.prp. No. 31 (1998–1999) *Om lov om erstatning ved pasientskader (pasientskadeloven) (Regarding Act Relating to Patient Injuries (Patient's Compensation Act))*, 73.
84. *See* https://www.npe.no/globalassets/dokumenter-pdf-og-presentasjoner/arsmelding/2021/arsrapport-2021-npeno.pdf (accessed 10 Jul. 2022, only in Norwegian).
85. *See* https://helseklage.no/forside/om-nasjonalt-klageorgan-for-helsetjenesten/tall-og-statistikk (accessed 10 July. 2022, only in Norwegian).

of this act' shall be punished by fines or a term of imprisonment not exceeding three months. HPA is here structured according to a traditional model, where the penal provision refers to all provisions of the act. There is a recent shift towards more targeted penalization, where the legislator has to specify which provisions in a given act that can be met with criminal responsibility.

167. The guilt requirement is either 'intentionally or by gross negligence'. This threshold implies that ordinary negligence that every professional may commit from time to time is not a criminal offence. An act or omission of 'gross negligence' must be very blameworthy and with a considerable reason for reproach, cf. the Penal Code section 23, second paragraph. In the preparatory work, the ministry paid a lot of attention on the system of liability and the division between civil and criminal liability.[86] As a starting point administrative measures and criminal liability are two separate systems with different aims and purposes, and thus containing different requirements of guilt and burden of proof. If the authorities are considering a withdrawal of authorization the aim is to protect patients, while a criminal sanction has different perspective (including general prevention). However, the ministry emphasizes that the total burden of criminal and civil liability should be taken into account to avoid an unreasonably hard measure for the health personnel concerned.

168. There have been several Supreme Court decisions concerning double jeopardy (*ne bis idem*) from various field, and a two cases against Norway was decided by the Grand Chamber of the European Court of Human Rights (*A v. Norway* (Appl. No. 24130/11) and *B v. Norway* (Appl. No. 29758/11), Judgment 15 November 2016). The Grand Chamber found that there was no violation of Article 4 of Protocol No. 7 to the Convention, and that the applicants had not been prosecuted and punished twice in respect of the same tax offence. The interrelationship between civil and criminal liability for health personnel has also been challenged. In Rt. 2004 p. 1343, a physician had been convicted to five months of imprisonment for attempt of robbery, violence against the police and use of narcotics. The prosecutor's claim for deprival of his position had been discharged. After the criminal procedure, the health authorities had suspended his licence (he was newly educated and thus having a licence and not an authorization). The Supreme Court held unanimously that it would not be a violation of European Convention on Human Rights (ECHR) Article 4 to Protocol 7 to suspend the licence based on the same factual circumstances leading to the criminal conviction. The legal departure of the assessment was the criteria formulated by the European Court of Human Rights (ECtHR) in the *Engel* case.[87] The main purpose of a suspension was to secure patient safety and the general public's confidence to physicians, which distinguished the administrative decision from the criminal procedure. Another issue was whether the discharge of the claim for deprival of his position should obstruct the health authorities from a subsequent suspension of licence. Some remarks in the preparatory work indicated that such a dualistic approach should not take place, but the majority (three judges)

86. Ot.prp. No. 13 (1998–1999) *Om lov om helsepersonell m v (helsepersonelloven) (Regarding Act Relating to Health Personnel (The Health Personnel Act)),* 161–198.
87. Appl. No. 5100/71, Judgment of 8 Jun. 1976.

put decisive weight to the open wording of the provision. The minority (two judges) found that the directives given in the preparatory work was clear and that it would have been unnecessarily complicated to regulate this kind of situation in the provision. The physician made an application to the European Court of Human Rights (ECtHR), claiming that the suspension of his licence to carry out duty services as a medical doctor constituted double jeopardy in breach of this Article 4 to Protocol 7.[88] The application was rejected as manifestly ill-founded pursuant to Article 35, third and fourth paragraph.

169. HPA is targeting 'anyone' ('den') and not only health personnel. In practice, most possible violation will be committed by health personnel, but non-professional may be charged if using titles or market health services cf. HPA section 74. In HR-2018-2452-A a retired consultant physician was given a fine of NOK 15,000 (approx. EUR 1,500) for violation of HPA section 67 cf. section 21a. The convicted person had been engaged as a private expert by an insurance company in a case between the company and claimant. Through his access to the hospital's computer system, he had acquired data from the claimant's medical record that he had not received from the insurance company. The Supreme Court found that the physician had acted with gross negligence. It concerned violation of a clear provision adopted several years earlier with the purpose of protecting patients' interests. The physician himself was highly educated and an experienced professional in an area where confidentiality is essential and where stricter requirements of due care apply. The reported cases from the High and City courts have been prosecutions against physicians as well as other health professionals. Most of the cases are stemming from different forms of sexual relations between the professional and the patient, and only a few are related to the professional conduct (gross negligence or breach of medical confidentiality).

170. According to HPA section 67, second paragraph public prosecution will only be instituted if it is in the public interest or by petition by the Norwegian Board of Health. The patient is not in the position to institute proceedings. He or she will not be considered as an 'aggravated party' according to the Criminal Procedure Code section 402, since the object of the criminal responsibility is to protect public interests and to obtain sufficient quality in the health services (*see* decision 8 June 2011 by Oslo District Court TOSLO-2011-28195).

171. Health personnel can also be held criminally responsible according to the Penal Code, for example, if committing sexual offences towards the patient. Such general provisions will not be dealt with here, but provisions with special interests for health professionals will be highlighted. The Penal Code section 209 is criminalizing obligations of confidentiality stipulated by law, such as HPA sections 21–29. Intentional breach of confidentiality as well as acts committed by gross negligence is punishable according to the Penal Code section 209. Assisted suicide is criminalized by section 277, but the provision leaves the court with discretion to

88. *Haarvig v. Norway*, Appl. No. 11187/05, decision 11 Dec. 2011; parts of the Supreme Court judgment is translated and cited in the decision.

impose milder punishment if special circumstances apply. Section 278 regulates compassionate homicide, and the court is also here vested with discretion to impose milder punishment.

172. The case reported in Rt. 2000 p. 646 is of interest. The case was decided under the Penal Code from 1902, but the legislation is substantially the same under the Penal Code from 2005. A physician had intentionally given lethal doses of morphine and ketogan to a patient with severe multiple sclerosis. The injection was given upon repeated and insisted requests from the patient, who was fully aware of the consequences. The physician unsuccessfully claimed that his acts were justified as an exceptional state of an emergency situation (the Penal Code 1902 section 48 stating that no person may be punished for any act committed to save someone's person form an otherwise unavoidable danger if the circumstances justified such an act, cf. the Penal Code 2005 section 17), alternatively that the act fell within the case law exemption of an exceptional necessity situation. The Supreme Court held that the legislator had made an informed choice when introducing milder punishment for assisted suicide and compassionate homicide, and not establishing an exemption from the criminal liability. This approach had also been supported in the legal literature and seemed to have broad support by the medical community. The Supreme Court also emphasized the distinction between the use of drugs in order to reduce pain in a terminal phase and the use of drugs with the aim of immediate terminating the life. The sentencing from the High Court was therefore upheld. Here, the physician was given suspended sentencing, with two years' probation (as well as a fine for omitting to keep a medical record of the incident).

III. Vicarious Liability

173. The Compensation Act regulates, *inter alia*, the employer's liability for injuries caused by the employees. An employer has a strict liability (liability without fault) for acts or omissions by his employees, cf. section 2-1. This liability applies also when the employee is a physician and the patient suffers the injury. Historically, many lawsuits were instituted against hospitals for negligence conducted by the physician. An illustrating example is the case reported in Rt. 1996 p. 1384. The state, as owner of a hospital, was sued and claimed responsible according to section 2-1. The plaintiff contended that the physicians had not provided properly follow-up treatment of complications after chemotherapy for brain cancer. The chemotherapy was administered through the groin, which had affected a nerve. The patient was complaining of pain after the surgery. His discomfort was presumed to be caused by other factors, before a surgery discovered the nerve in squeeze. The crux of the matter was whether any employee had acted out of negligence. According to established case law this includes both active intervention and omissions, and it is not necessary for the plaintiff to identify wrongs by a specific employee. The majority (four judges) held that it was difficult to make reliable diagnosis in situations where the patient had imprecise pain in the crotch and the physicians had not acted out of negligence. The minority (one judge) held that the patient's pain was timely so closely connected to the administration of the chemotherapy that the physicians would be obliged to a further continuous observation.

174. After the introduction of the scheme of compensation after patient injuries, first by agreement, then by statutory provisions (*see supra* Chapter 4, §1, I), lawsuits towards hospitals or institutions are rare. For claims of compensation against the state, health enterprises, counties and municipalities, the compensation scheme is compulsory for incidents falling within the scope of the act, cf. the Patient's Compensation Act section 5.

§2. Quality Assurance

175. Different legal tools for securing a sufficient quality of the health services are stipulated in the legislation, both targeting the individual professional and the system as a whole. The requirements are found in regulation both on a primary and specialized level, as well as in the legislation concerning the profession and in specific branches.

176. According to the Health and Care Services Act section 4-1, health and care services that are offered or provided pursuant to this Act must be conducted responsibly. The municipality shall organize the services such that:

(a) each patient or healthcare user is offered comprehensive and coordinated health and care services;
(b) each patient or healthcare user is offered worthy services;
(c) the health and care service and personnel who provide the services are able to comply with their statutory duties; and
(d) adequate expertise for the services is ensured.

These directives are both focusing on the services provided to the individual patient (litra a and b) and focusing on the obligations of the provider on a more general level (litra c and d). The newly introduced section 4-2a (by law of 7 June 2013 No. 29) is combining these two perspectives by obliging the municipality to ensure that the patient is provided with relevant information pursuant to PRA section 3-2 (and to the next of kin pursuant to PRA section 3-3). Section 4-2a was introduced as part of a larger reform to strengthen the legal position of patients and their next of kin.[89] Section 4-2 is targeting everyone who provides services pursuant to the act. They 'must ensure that the activities work systematically towards quality improvements and patient and healthcare user safety'. The ministry is entitled to provide further directives by regulations. Such regulations are not yet given, but the regulations made under the former legislation are still in force, cf. the life-prolonging clause in

89. Prop. 100 L (2013–2014) *Endringer i pasient- og brukerrettighetsloven mv. (styrking av pasienters, brukeres og pårørendes stilling m.m.) (Amendments to the Patient's and User's Act, Etc. (Strengthening of the Position of Patients, Users and Next of Kin, Etc.)).*

section 13-2. More detailed provisions on quality in primary health and care services are found in regulation of 27 June 2003 No. 792.

177. Turning to specialized health services, Specialized Health Care Act section 3-4 stipulates that any health institution who provides services pursuant to this act shall establish quality and patients' safety bodies as part of the systematic work which the institution is obliged to carry out according to section 2-1a, third paragraph (the obligation to plan, implement, evaluate and correct the work in the institution so that the services are in accordance with acts and regulations) and section 3-4a (quality improvement and patients' safety). The institution is according to section 3-10 obliged to ensure that employed personnel is given such education and training so that they can provide services of sufficient standard and quality.

178. Since other parts of the legislation, more in detail, are stipulating quality requirements, the HPA is rather briefly on this matter. According to section 16 every facility providing health and care services shall 'be organized in such a way that health personnel are able to comply with their statutory duties'. The ministry is given the competence to stipulate by regulation further provision on the organization of facilities providing health and care services and on internal control, cf. HPA section 16, second paragraph. The Health Supervision Act is also rather briefly due to the requirements in other parts of the regulation. According to section 5 every facility providing health and care services shall establish a system of internal control and ensure that the services are planned, implemented and maintained according to requirements stipulated by law or regulations. Such provisions are given by regulation of 28 October 2016 No. 1250.

179. Moving to more specific branches professionals or institutions conducting research activity must have a system of internal control which must be carried out in a manner that is adapted 'to the size, nature activities and risk factors if the research', cf. the Health Research Act 6, second paragraph. The ministry is given the competence to stipulate further provision by regulation concerning the organization of medical and health research, requirements concerning the research protocol and 'concerning internal control', cf. section 6, third paragraph.

180. The regulations regarding quality control are found in several provisions and it can be difficult to obtain an overview of the legal situations. This is partly due to the legislative approach where rather parallel provisions are found in the regulations on different levels, as well in legislation regulation different branches. The aim of this dualistic approach is to have a kind of pedagogic legislation, where the providers can find their duties in their 'local' regulations. The downside of this method is a rather complex regulation, although the different provisions are rarely conflicting. Another particularity is the form of indirect review by internal control. Although supervision bodies are given the competence also to take steps after incidents have occurred, cf. *infra* §3, a core mechanism is the activity to be taken by the entities themselves, both in order to provide sufficient services to each individual patient and to ensure the quality in general. The role of the supervision bodies is in this perspective not to go into individual cases but to review the internal system as such. Another feature is the triple approach, where the regulations are both targeting the patient (as receiver of health services), the health professional (as individual provider) and the entities (as an institutional provider).

§3. Review Boards

181. There are several bodies having some kind of role in supervising the provision of health services. The Norwegian Board of Health Supervision is a national public institution organized under the Ministry of Health and Care Services.[90] Their legal foundation is the Health Supervision Act. The board is led by a director, appointed by the government. The board is organized in two levels. Besides the national level, the regional level is the county. Each county shall have a county physician, cf. section 3, third paragraph. In addition to their supervision role in the field of health and care services, the Norwegian Board of Health Supervision is also responsible for supervision of childcare services. The supervision authorities work independently of political management. To a large extent, they decide themselves which services to give priority to with regard to supervision, and which areas supervision shall include. Among other things, priorities are determined on the basis of information about risk and vulnerability.

182. The county governor shall conduct supervision of health and care services within the county, as well of all personnel providing health and care services, cf. section 4, second paragraph. The county governor shall notify the Norwegian Board of Health Supervision of circumstances that may lead to a warning, a withdrawal or suspension of authorization, licence or specialist approval according to HPA section 11. The decision in such cases is vested with the Norwegian Board of Health Supervision, cf. section 10. If a facility providing health or care services is run in a manner that may cause injuries or in other aspects are acting out of negligence, the Norwegian Board of Health Supervision can issue directives aiming at correcting the misconduct, cf. section 8. The legislation also contains the possibility of imposing a coercive fine in certain circumstances (*see* paragraph 215 *infra* for an example), cf. section 9.

183. An important aspect of the supervision is the information flow to the supervision bodies. According to the Health Supervision Act section 3-3 entities providing health and care services shall immediate notify the Health Directorate of Health of incidents leading to death or with significant personal injury or if one patient is harming another. Such notifications shall not include data that can reveal the identity of the persons involved and cannot lead to sanctions against involved personnel. According to the Specialized Health Care Act section 3-3a institutions covered by the act shall immediately notify deaths or very serious injury of patients the Norwegian Board of Health supervision and to the State Investigating Commission for Health and Care Services, cf. Act 16 June 2017 No. 56. Also, situations where one

90. For a presentation of the board's tasks in English, *see* https://www.helsetilsynet.no/en/ (accessed 1 Mar. 2019).

patient is harming another shall be reported according to this provision. The duty to notify is limited to situations where the outcome in unexpected due to the risk.

184. Turning to the individual health personnel they are obliged – of their own record – to provide information to the supervising authorities on matters that 'may endanger patient safety', cf. HPA section 17. However, such information shall not reveal information that is subject to medical confidentiality. The obligation to report according to HPA section 17 must be seen in conjunction with other provisions. According to HPA section 30, health personnel shall – upon request – give information to supervision authorities regardless of medical confidentiality. Besides the provisions in HPA, the general regulations concerning the relationship between the undertaking and the employee apply. According to the Working Environment Act section 2-4, an employee has 'a right' to 'notify concerning censurable conditions at the undertaking' ('whistle blowing'). Further requirements on the procedure and burden of proof are given in the working environment act, which also stipulates a protection against retaliation in connection with notification (section 2-5). Health personnel may also be obliged to inform patients about unwanted incidents (*see* paragraph 205 *infra*).

185. The information flow is also a question of communication from the supervision authorities. The Norwegian Board of Health Supervision shall inform the health personnel's employer of warnings, withdrawal, voluntary revoke, or suspension of authorization, licence and specialist approval, cf. the HPA section 66. Such information shall also be given to authorities in other countries according to obligations under international law.

186. The Parliamentary Ombudsperson (for the patient's ombudsperson, cf. paragraph 243 *infra*) supervises public administration agencies, cf. the Parliamentary Ombudsperson Act. Supervision is carried out on the basis of complaints from citizens concerning any maladministration or injustice on the part of a public agency. The Ombudsman may also address issues on his own initiative, cf. section 15. The Ombudsman is entitled to express his opinions on matters within his responsibility. The administration will normally follow up his opinions, but they are not formally bound by such statements. Since most health personnel either are employed by public entities or are having an agreement with public entities, issues concerning health personnel will often fall within the sphere of the responsibility of the Parliamentary Ombudsperson. Complaints from health personnel (as well from patients) are on a regular basis reviewed by the Ombudsperson. An example is the opinion of 25 September 2014 (Case SOM-2014-379). A physician employed in the municipality had made statements in the local newspaper where he criticized reductions in public spending to health services and the shutdown of nursing home beds. He was given a reprimand from the municipality for disloyalty. The Ombudsperson held that the imposed sanction was an unjustified interference in the freedom of speech.

187. As an element in the efficiency improvement of the public sector and in order to have more patient-oriented services the government introduced a new organization of the central health administration.[91] A new national complaint body for health services has been established (and situated in Bergen, outside the capital). The administration of the Patients' Injury Compensation Board (*see supra* paragraph 154), the Appeals Board for Health Personnel (*see supra* paragraph 85), as well as other bodies were united in one administrative entity (the boards will continue with their task).

§4. DISCIPLINARY ORGANIZATIONS

I. Order of Physicians

188. The Norwegian Medical Association (established in 1886) holds the position both as a professional association and as a trade union for Norwegian physicians.[92] The association has nearly 35,000 members, and approximately 95% of the physicians in Norway are Members of the Norwegian Medical Association (MNMA). The main aims of the Norwegian Medical Association are to secure the professional, social and financial interests of the members to promote their interests in matters concerning medical education, professional development and scientific activities, and to advance the quality of the Norwegian healthcare system, cf. the statutes section 1-2. Membership of the association entitles to use the initials MNMA. Approved specialists are also registered in medical societies according to their specialization. The association's chief decision-making body is the representative body, which decides the overall policy of the association and the annual budget. The Central Board has nine members including the President and Vice-President of the Association and is elected every second year by the representative body.

II. Professional Codes

189. The code of ethics for physicians was introduced in 1962, and is subsequently amended, most recently in 2015.[93] The Medical Ethics Council is the association's highest authority on medical ethical issues. The rule of procedure is given by the representative body. The council consists of chair, vice chair and three other members, elected by the representative body for a four-year term, cf. section 3. One of the association's lawyers is secretary for the council. Cases regarding the professional part of medical services fall outside the scope of the council, cf. section 2.

91. Prop. 9 L (2015–2016) *Endringer i helselovgivningen (Nasjonalt klageorgan for helsetjenesten mv.) (Amendments in the Health Law Regulation (National Complaint Body for Health Services)).*
92. *See* https://www.legeforeningen.no (accessed 10 Jul. 2022, only in Norwegian).
93. *See* https://www.legeforeningen.no/om-oss/etikk/etiske-regler-koder-deklarasjoner-og-lignende/etiske-regler-for-leger/ (accessed 10 July. 2019, only in Norwegian).

According to the same provision, the council will normally not examine cases that are under judicial or administrative review.

190. The main aim of the council is to be an adviser for the association's members, the association's bodies and the society, cf. section 2. The council is both expounding issues of medical ethics in general and is deciding cases based on individual complaints on physician's conduct. The council decisions are binding for the members of the association, and cannot be overruled by other bodies of the organization. If the council is of the opinion that a physician is in breach of the code of ethics, it can express its disapproval or reprimand the doctor. The council may require that the doctor apologizes for and/or discontinues the matter for which he or she is reproached, and it may also propose to the Executive Committee that the doctor is excluded from the association.

191. The code of ethics for physicians is divided into five parts. Part 1 contains regular provisions, including the general object of the physician to 'cure, alleviate and console' (section 1, first paragraph). The physician shall build his or her profession on 'respect for fundamental human rights' (section 1, second paragraph). The provisions are partly reiterating patient's rights (right to information, discretion, etc.). Some provisions are emphasizing the physician's particular responsibility. Section 7 dictates the prohibition on 'sexual, economic and religious' exploitation and stresses also that a patient's consent from the patient does not absolve the physician of responsibility. According to section 5, a physician shall not perform active euthanasia or assisted suicide. Several provisions target financial aspects. According to section 12, second paragraph a physician must not enter into relations with the pharmaceutical industry or providers of medical equipment that may be detrimental to the confidence in the doctor's professional assessments.

192. Part 2 contains rules regarding the conduct between the physician and his or her colleagues and collaborators. If a physician who discovers signs of professional or ethical laxity by a colleague and collaborator, he or she should directly address the person concerned, cf. section 1. A physician should take care not to criticize colleagues and collaborators when speaking to patients and their relatives, cf. section 5. Practices with regard to referrals must not be governed by financial interests, cf. section 8.

193. Part 3 contains rules regarding marketing and other dissemination about the physician's services. According to section 1, first paragraph marketing and other disseminations should only contain information about:

- the location, opening hours, and administration of the practice;
- the type of practice, speciality and title of the practitioner;
- diagnostic and therapeutic methods; and
- the fees charged.

194. Marketing and other dissemination must not mention possible or expected results of specific services, or the quality of the services, cf. section 1, third paragraph. No formulations may be used which could give the public the impression that by failing to avail oneself of the services advertised, one is placing one's own or other persons' somatic, mental or social health at risk, cf. section 1, third paragraph. A physician may not promote or market medicines or medical consumer goods, cf. section 5. Mention in professional medical contexts in articles, lectures and the like, not made for gain, is – according to the wording of the provision – not regarded as marketing.

195. Part 3 contains rules regarding physician's issuing of certificates and medical reports. A physician shall not issue a medical report if he or she is questioning one's own impartiality, cf. section 2. A medical report shall rely on collection of necessary information and on such comprehensive examination as necessary for the purpose, cf. section 4. A medical report shall contain sufficient information to serve its purpose and should in its wording be objective and neutral, cf. section 4.

196. The Medical Ethics Council publishes their annual reports on the association's website (in Norwegian only). In 2021, the council held seven meetings and reviewed sixty-one cases, in which they made a decision in twenty-one (forty-one cases where struck of the list of various reasons, *inter alia*, considered to address the professional part of medical services or considered as purely legal issues). The council is also submitting their opinions in cases on public hearings (typically drafts for new regulations).

197. An ongoing debate in Norway is concerning euthanasia, cf. the Code of Ethics Part 1, section 5. The representative body turned down a proposition of amendments to this provision in 2014. As a follow up, the council organized a seminar on the topic in 2014. The issue was then put on the agenda of the representative body in 2015. The Code of Ethics Part 1, section 5 was supplemented with a new sentence. According to this 'withdrawing or not initiating futile treatment (limitation of treatment) shall not be considered as euthanasia'.

III. Biomedical Ethics Committee

198. Besides the separate legislation concerning medical research (cf. *infra* paragraph 337), there were until recently no statutory obligation for health services to organize ethics committees. However, the state had as owner of the regional enterprises instructed them to establish such committees. The first initiative came in the 1970s from the ethical council of the Norwegian Medical Association, and the idea was taken up again in the beginning of the 1990s. Test committees were established at three hospitals, where a core idea was that the committees should be interdisciplinary and working after a 'bottom up' approach by engaging health personnel with direct contact with the patient. The try out was evaluated and considered a success leading up to a political decision. According to the steering documents of the regional health enterprises for 2003 all of them should within the end of 2004 establish clinical ethics committees.

199. The Specialists Health Care Act was amended on 7 May 2022. Section 2-4a makes it mandatory for the health enterprises to establish clinical ethics committees. According to the legislation the committee shall contribute to increase healthcare personnel's ability to identify, analyse and clarify ethical issues regarding patient's treatment and priority of resources. Upon request from health personnel or patients the committee can also assist with advice concerning actual ethical challenges. Also the patient's next of kin can ask for advice, if this is to be considered to be in line with the wish of the patient.

200. The provision also includes directives on the composition and procedure. It is required that clinical ethics are multidisciplinary and include patient's representative as a member. If possible, members shall have competence in medical ethics and in health law committee. The committee shall conduct its tasks in an independent manner.

Part II. The Physician-Patient Relationship

Chapter 1. General Description

§1. Rights and Duties of Physicians and Patients

201. The basic structure concerning the physician and patient relationship is that the rights of the patients are laid down in the PRA, while the duties of the physician are laid down in the HPA. The latter also include rights and duties of the physician towards the health authorities and the society in general. The object of the PRA is to 'help ensure that all citizens have equal access to good quality healthcare' by 'granting patients rights' in their relation with the health services, cf. section 1-1, first paragraph. The provisions of the HPA shall help to 'promote a relationship between the patient and the health service' and safeguard 'respect for life, integrity and human dignity' of each patient, cf. section 1-1, second paragraph. According to the preparatory work, the object of the act shall function as a guideline when interpreting the act.[94] The purpose of HPA is to 'contribute to safety for patients' and 'quality within the health service' as well as trust 'in both health personnel and the health service', cf. section 1.

202. The PRA section 1-3 contains definitions for the purposes of this act. These definitions are to a large extent either referred to in other parts of the regulations, or reiterated in other acts. A 'patient' is in litra a) defined as a person 'who contacts the health and care services requesting healthcare', or to 'whom the health and care services provides or offers healthcare'. The definition is rather broad, and the status as patient is obtained even when seeking services. Additionally, care services are now also included (cf. *supra* paragraph 54). The definition of 'patient' must be read in conjunction with the definition of 'healthcare' in litra c). This comprises of 'acts which have a preventive, diagnostic therapeutic health preserving or rehabilitating effect and are carried out by health personnel for the purposes of nursing and care'. This definition is interrelated with the definition of health personnel, which is not stipulated in the PRA which in this respect refers to the definition in HPA section 3. This definition is rather confusing regarding other professions, but for physicians it includes everyone with an authorization or licence. The 'health and care services' are defined in PRA section 1-3 litra d) as 'the municipal health and care service, the specialist health service, the dental health service and private providers of health

94. Ot.prp. No. 12 (1998–1999) *Lov om pasientrettigheter (pasientrettighetsloven) (Act Relating to Patient's Right (The Patient's Right Act))*, 125.

and care providers'. Many of the definitions in section 1-1 are rather broad. Since they to a large extent are interrelated by building on each other, the total outcome is that many professionals are included as 'health personnel' and that many citizens will be considered as 'patients' in different situations. The definitions are frequently amended in order to keep pace with the development. However, the definitions are of limited relevance when interpreting the provisions of the act.[95] The exception is the patient's next of kin, which will be elaborated in the next paragraph.

203. Prior to the PRA, the patient's next of kin was playing a minor role in the health regulations. The PRA lead to the strengthening of the legal position of the patient's relatives, which will be dealt with under the relevant material and procedural rules. As a consequence, the PRA also contains a definition of 'next of kin' and the closest 'next of kin', cf. section 1-1, litra b). The definition of these two alternatives is the same, but many provisions vest competence to *the closest* 'next of kin'. The primary alternative in the definition is the person who is named by the patient. The patient's selection must not be made in writing, but it is preferably to be documented in the medical records. There is no regulation regarding the appointed person's acceptance of the task, but it is not an obligation to take such a position. Unwilling persons will therefore be excluded. If the patient is incapable of naming his or her next of kin, the next of kin shall be the person who 'to the greatest extent' has had 'lasting and continuous' contact with the patient, based on order of appearance in the text of the provision. They can be grouped into three (with priority as mentioned also within the group). The first group is those with an emotional relationship (spouse, partner and cohabitant), the second group is those with family relationships (children, parents, siblings, grandparents or other family members) and the third group is those with a legal relationship (guardian warden with competence in personal matters). A special regulation is made for psychiatric patients, cf. the last sentence in the definition in litra c). In cases of involuntary observation or involuntary admittance according to the Mental Health Care Act, the person who to the greatest extent has had lasting and continuous contact with the patient is entitled to the rights as the closest next of kin according to and the Mental Health Care Act, unless specific reasons are against this. The background of this specific regulation is according to the preparatory work to address situation where the patient has a serious mental disorder and where there is no rational motivation for the patient's choice.[96]

---

95. *See* Aslak Syse, *Pasient- og brukerrettighetsloven med kommentarer (The Patient- and User Act – A Commentary)* 151 (4th ed., Gyldendal 2015).
96. Ot.prp. No. 65 (2005–2006) *Om lov om endringer i psykisk helsevernloven og pasientrettighetsloven m.v. (Regarding Act Relating to Amendments of the Mental Health Care Act and the Patient's Rights Act),* 43–44.

§2. INFORMED CONSENT

204. The PRA Chapter 4 contains provisions regarding consent to healthcare.[97] According to section 4-1, first paragraph healthcare 'may only be provided' with the patient's consent, unless 'legal authority exists' or there 'are other valid grounds' for providing healthcare without consent. In order for 'the consent to be valid', the patient must have received 'necessary information' concerning his health condition and the content of the healthcare. Provisions regarding the right to participation and information are stipulated in Chapter 3. The provisions in PRA Chapters 3 and 4 are general and cover all kinds of healthcare, unless exceptions are found in other parts of the legislation.

205. The patient's right to participation is elaborated in section 3-1. The patient is 'entitled' to participate in the implementation of their health and care services. This includes the patient's right to 'choose between available and medically sound methods of examination and treatment'. The form of participation shall be 'adapted to the individual's ability to give and receive information'. If the patient is not able to give consent, the patient's closest next of kin is 'entitled to participate together with the patient', cf. section 3-1, third paragraph. If the patient wishes other persons to be present when health and care services are provided, his or her wishes 'shall be accommodated as far as possible'.

206. The patient's right to information is elaborated in section 3-2. According to the preparatory work the object of this right is three-folded.[98] First, to enable the patient to take care of their own interest. Second, information is a prerequisite for consent. Third, information is necessary in order to participate in an effective way. The patient 'shall have the information that is necessary to obtain an insight' into his or her health condition and the content of the healthcare. The patient 'shall also be informed of possible risks and side effects'. The preparatory works do not refer to earlier case law, but it is considered that previous judgments are still giving some guidance.[99] In Rt. 1993 p. 1169, a patient claimed compensation for lack of information prior to a surgery. The physicians anticipated that he had a benign tumour on his lung and recommended surgery. The surgery was carried out and the tumour turned out to be a neuroma. The removal of the neuroma caused different forms of functional loss. The patient claimed that he was given insufficient information prior to the surgery and that the consent was not valid due to objective incorrect diagnosis. The Supreme Court held that consequences which are not likely to occur, but where the risk is manifest, presents the physicians of a difficult challenge. The diagnosis was fully reasonable, and it was not practicable to interrupt the surgery when

97. For an in-depth analysis of the Norwegian legislation, *see* Henriette Sinding Aasen, *Pasientens rett til selvbestemmelse ved medisinsk behandling (The Patient's Right to Self Determination in Cases of Medical Treatment)* 279–472 (Fagbokforlaget 2000) and Marit Halvorsen, *Rettslige grunnlag for medisinsk behandling (Legal Basis for Medical Treatment)* (Fagbokforlaget 1998).

98. Ot.prp. No. 12 (1998–1999) *Lov om pasientrettigheter (pasientrettighetsloven) (Act Relating to Patient's Right (The Patient's Right Act)),* 69.

99. Compare Aslak Syse, *Pasient- og brukerrettighetsloven med kommentarer (The Patient- and User Rights Act – A Commentary)* 359 (4th ed., Gyldendal 2015).

discovering the neuroma. The patient's claim for compensation was thus rejected (separate opinion of one judge). In Rt. 1998 p. 1538, a patient underwent surgery in order to treat or alleviate his back afflictions. Some of the nerves were damaged, inflicting his sexual abilities. The Supreme Court held that the information given to the patient did not include an assessment of the possible side effects. Nevertheless, his claim for compensation was turned down since it was presumed that he would have consented to the surgery regardless of sufficient information (two judges dissented on this point). However, it must be kept in mind the development of patient's rights in recent years. The outcome in the two mentioned cases would therefore necessarily not be the same today. In the preparatory work, the necessity to inform patients of unlikely risks are stressed, in order to avoid unnecessary complains after intervention.[100]

207. According to section 3-2, second paragraph information shall not be given against the expressed will of the patient, unless it is 'necessary in order to prevent harmful effects caused by the healthcare', or it is prescribed by or pursuant to statute. The legislation regarding communicable diseases is often used as an example of such a deviating provision. According to the Communicable Disease Act section 2-1, the physician 'shall' inform the patient about the communicable disease and the way it spreads and personal guidance in preventive measures. PRA section 3-2, third paragraph states that information may be omitted if it is 'absolutely necessary in order to prevent endangering the patient's life or serious damage to the patient's health'. Information may also be omitted if it is 'clearly inadvisable to provide such information out of consideration for persons who are close to the patient'. The ministry emphasizes in the preparatory work that the threshold for omitting information must be high.[101] It must also be taken into consideration that the knowledge of information being concealed may itself be harmful for the patient. The provision regarding omitting information must be read in conjunction with the regulations regarding access to medical records (*see* §6 *infra*).

208. PRA section 3-2, fourth, fifth and sixth paragraphs contain provisions on information to the patient as part of a follow-up of certain unwanted outcomes. If 'injury or serious complications are inflicted upon the patient', the patient 'shall be informed of this', cf. PRA section 3-2, fourth paragraph. At the same time, the patient 'shall be made aware of his or her right to apply for compensation through the Norwegian System of Compensation to Patients'. Simultaneously, the patient shall be informed of the right to address the Patient's Ombudsman as well as supervision bodies. If 'injury or serious complications are inflicted upon the patient', and the outcome is unforeseen based on expected risk, the patient shall be informed of which measures the health services will implement in order to avoid similar incidents in the future, cf. section 3-2, fifth paragraph. If, after the treatment has been

100. Ot.prp. No. 12 (1998–1999), 70.
101. Ot.prp. No. 12 (1998–1999) *Lov om pasientrettigheter (pasientrettighetsloven) (Act Relating to Patient's Right (The Patient's Right Act)),* 71.

concluded, it is discovered that the patient may have 'suffered considerable injury as a result of the healthcare', the patient shall be informed of this if possible, cf. section 3-2, sixth paragraph.

209. Information to the patient's next of kin is stipulated in PRA section 3-3. If the patient consents thereto or 'circumstances justify it', the patient's next of kin shall receive information concerning the patient's health condition and the healthcare that is being provided, cf. section 3-3, first paragraph. The alternative 'circumstances justify it' is rather vague, but will in a normal situation allow health personnel to pass on information, unless the patient beforehand has objected to this. If the patient is over 16 years of age and 'obviously incapable of safeguarding his or her own interests due to a physical or mental disorder, senile dementia or mental retardation', section 3-3, second paragraph stipulates that both the patient and his or her closest next of kin are entitled to information pursuant to the provisions of section 3-2. If the patient dies and this outcome is unforeseen based on expected risk, the patient's next of kin is entitled to information according to section 3-2, fourth and fifth paragraphs, as long as the medical confidentiality is not an impediment, cf. section 3-3, last paragraph.

210. Section 3-5 contains requirements regarding the form of information. Information shall be adapted to the 'qualifications of the individual recipient, such as age, maturity, experience and cultural and linguistic background'. The information shall be provided in a 'considerate manner'. As far as possible, health personnel 'shall ensure that the patient has understood the contents and significance' of the information. An entry concerning the information that has been provided 'shall be made in the patient's medical records'. Special challenges occur when an increasing number of patients have a foreign linguistic and cultural background, and there is both a lack of competent translators and inappropriate use of family members as translators.[102] The PAA has been amended, introducing a prohibition against using children of as interpreters, *cf.* section 11e (amendment 10 June 2016 No. 23).[103] Administrative agencies shall not use children to 'interpret or otherwise communicate information between the administration and persons who lack sufficient language skills to communicate directly with the administration'. Exceptions may be made when necessary 'to avoid loss of life or serious damage to health, or when necessary in other emergency situations'. Exceptions may also be made in circumstances when 'it must be deemed judicious, having regard to the interest of the child and the other circumstances of the case'. The regulation is general, but will especially be of relevance in the healthcare sector, as well as in immigration cases.

102. *See* NOU 2014:8 *Tolking i offentlig sektor – et spørsmål om rettssikkerhet og likeverd (Interpretation within Public Sector – A Question about Rule of Law and Equality)* 53–60 (with an English summary).
103. Prop. 65 L (2015–2016) *Endringer i forvaltningsloven (forbud mot bruk av barn som tolk) (Amendments to the Public Administration Act (Prohibition on the Use of Children as Interpreter)).*

211. Turning back to the consent requirement, the consent may be given 'explicitly or tacitly', cf. section 4-2, first paragraph. A written consent is therefore unnecessary, except for specific situation where such a requirement is stipulated in the regulation (*see infra* paragraph 274 regarding sterilization as an example). The provision also regulates in which situation a tacit consent is valid. It must be 'probable', based on 'the patient's conduct and all other circumstances', that he or she accepts the healthcare. Tacit consent is practical in every day situation, typically where the patient takes a medicine after receiving sufficient information on effects and side effects. In some situations, it is advisable for the physician to document the consent and the information given, typically in cases of particular risk or pain. The patient 'may withdraw' his consent, cf. section 4-1, second paragraph. If the patient withdraws consent, the healthcare provider 'shall give the necessary information' regarding the consequences of not giving the healthcare.

212. Section 4-3 regulates who has competence to give consent. According to litra a) every person of 'full legal age and legal capacity', unless special provisions dictate otherwise (for exceptions, *see, inter alia, infra* 274 regarding sterilization). Litra b) states that minors over 16 years of age are able to give a valid consent, unless special provisions or the nature of the measure dictate otherwise (*see infra* Chapter 2, §2). Competence to give consent 'may cease to apply wholly or partly' if the patient, on 'account of a physical or mental disorder, senile dementia or mental retardation', is 'clearly incapable' of understanding what the consent entails. It is a kind of strange regulatory approach, where general criteria are mixed with specific conditions, although the latter are rather practical. Nevertheless, the wording of the provision explicitly states that the threshold for not being competent is high ('clearly incapable'). This condition is a substantial rule as well as a burden of proof rule. The assessment of competence has to be concrete, based on the individual patient's condition just now (which may change during a day or in near future). Furthermore, the assessment can depend upon kind of intervention, i.e., surgery with a risk of a fatal outcome contra routine blood samples.

213. According to PRA section 4-3, third paragraph, the healthcare provider shall decide whether the patient lacks competence to consent pursuant to the second paragraph. Based on the 'patient's age, mental state, maturity and experience', health personnel shall do their best to enable the patient himself or herself to consent to healthcare. A decision concerning lack of competence to give consent shall 'state the reasons' for the decision and 'shall be given in writing', and 'if possible' shall immediately be present to the patient and his or her closest next of kin, cf. section 4-3, fourth paragraph. If the patient has no next of kin, the decision shall be presented to qualified health personnel.

214. PRA sections 4-6–4-8 contain provisions regarding representation of adult patients without the competence to consent (for children, *see infra* Chapter 2, §1). If a patient who is of full legal age and legal capacity is not competent to give consent, the healthcare provider may make decisions concerning healthcare that is 'not of a highly invasive nature with regard to its extent and duration', cf. section 4-6, first paragraph. Healthcare that is of a highly invasive nature may be provided if it is 'deemed to be in the patient's best interests', and 'it is likely that the patient would have given permission for such care', cf. section 4-6, second paragraph. If possible, information should be obtained from the patient's next of kin in order to determine what the patient would have wanted. The competence to decide healthcare pursuant to section 4-6, second paragraph is vested with health personnel who provide healthcare, in collaboration with other qualified health personnel. It shall be documented in the patient's medical records what information has been obtained from the patient's closest next of kin and the opinion of other qualified health personnel, cf. section 4-6, second paragraph, fourth sentence. Healthcare according to section 4-6, first and second paragraphs cannot be provided if the patient objects thereto, unless other provisions dictate otherwise. Originally, PRA section 4-6, second paragraph vested the competence to the patient's next of kin, but the provision was amended in 2006 (law of 22 December 2006 No. 99). The ministry stated that the patient's next of kin originally was given a responsibility that was too burdensome and that it was appropriate that such decisions were taken by health personnel.[104]

215. A specific tool was amended to PRA in 2013 (law of 14 June 2013 No. 36). The health and care services may take decision regarding use of technical devises for alerting and localization as part of health and care services to patients over the age of 18 years being without competence to consent, cf. section 4-6a. A practical example will be GPS tagging of elderly patients suffering from dementia. The intervention must be 'necessary' in order to avoid or limit risk of injuries to the patient and be in the patient's interest. The provision contains further requirements and does also explicitly state that the use of devices is excluded where the patient objects thereto. The amendment was motivated by a clarification of the legal basis, and the preparatory works contain an analysis of the conformity with various human rights instruments.[105]

216. Patients who have been declared legally incapacitated in personal matters pursuant to the Guardianship Act shall, to 'the greatest possible extent', consent to healthcare himself or herself, cf. section 4-7. If this is not possible, the guardian may give consent on behalf of the legally incapacitated person.

217. While the before mentioned provisions in PRA Chapter 4 regulate the consent in various aspects, section 4-9 regulates the patient's right to refuse healthcare in three special situations. The legislator introduced section 4-9 as a response to situations that occurred from time to time prior to the PRA, and where the current

104. Ot.prp. No. 64 (2005–2006) *Om lov om endringar i pasientrettslova og biobanklova (helsehjelp og forsking – personar utan samtykkekompetanse) (Regarding Act Relating to Amendments to the Patient's Rights Act and the Biobank Act (Health Care and Research – Persons without Competence to Consent)),* 15–18.

105. Prop. 90 L (2012–2013) *Endringer i pasient- og brukerrettighetsloven mv. (bruk av varslings- og lokaliseringsteknologi) (Amendments to the Patient's and User's Rights Act, Etc. (Use of Alert and Localization Technology)).*

legal situation was supposed to be out of pace with the opinion of the general public.[106] *First*, the patient is entitled, 'due to serious conviction', to refuse to receive 'blood or blood products'. Even though the term 'serious conviction' encompasses religious, political and philosophical belief, this alternative is for all practical matters addressing member of Jehovah's witnesses, where the reluctance to blood and blood products is deeply rooted in their religious beliefs. The patient's entitlement according to this provision applies even if the outcome is fatal. It is somewhat strange that this rather particular situation is dealt with first in the provision, which must be seen in light of the then contemporary discussion. *Second*, the patient is entitled to refuse to 'break off an ongoing hunger strike', also on the condition 'due to serious conviction'. *Third*, a dying patient is entitled to object to life-prolonging treatment. This alternative will be elaborated *infra* in Chapter 2, §3. Section 4-9, third paragraph stipulates common conditions for the three situations where the patient is entitled to refuse healthcare. Health personnel must 'make sure' that the patient as mentioned in first and second paragraph is 'of full legal age' and is not been declared legally incapacitated in personal matters pursuant to the Guardianship Act. Parents can therefore not refuse blood or blood products on behalf of their patients. Furthermore, health personnel must make sure that the patient has been given 'adequate information' and has 'understood the consequences of refusing treatment' for his and her own health.

218. PRA section 4-1 states that healthcare may only be provided based on the patient's consent, unless 'legal authority exists or there are other valid legal grounds for providing healthcare without consent'. A presentation of the exceptions given in the legislation will be given in the forthcoming text. PRA Chapter 4A contains provisions on healthcare for patients without competence to give consent who object to healthcare.[107] The amendment was made to clarify – and to some extent expand – the legal basis for involuntary intervention, in order to provide a better legal protection for the patients.[108] The provisions in the chapter apply regardless of diagnosis, but a main target group is elderly patients suffering from dementia. The amendment was disputed, and in the preparatory work the ministry makes an assessment of conformity with various human rights instruments.[109] The object of the provisions in Chapter 4A is to provide 'necessary healthcare in order to prevent significant harm to health and to prevent and limit the use of force', cf. section 4A-1, first paragraph. Healthcare shall be provided in such a way as to ensure 'respect for the individual's physical and mental integrity', and 'shall as far as possible be in

---

106. Ot.prp. No. 12 (1998–1999) *Lov om pasientrettigheter (pasientrettighetsloven) (Act Relating to Patient's Right (The Patient's Right Act))*, 87–88.
107. For an in-depth analysis of the provisions in the PRA Ch. 4, *see* Bjørn Henning Østenstad, *Heimelsspørsmål i behandling og omsorg overfor psykisk utviklingshemma og aldersdemente (Questions Regarding the Legal Basis for Treatment and Care of Mentally Disabled and Elderly with Dementia)* (Fagbokforlaget 2011).
108. Ot.prp. No. 64 (2005–2006) *Om lov om endringar i pasientrettslova og biobanklova (helsehjelp og forsking – personar utan samtykkekompetanse) (Regarding Act Relating to Amendments to the Patient's Rights Act and the Biobank Act (Health Care and Research – Persons without Competence to Consent))*, 5.
109. Ot.prp. No. 64 (2005–2006), 67–70.

keeping with the patient's right to self-determination', cf. section 4A-1, second paragraph. The provisions in Chapter 4A apply when health personnel provide healthcare to 'patients over 16 years of age who lack competence to give consent', and 'who object to the healthcare', *cf.* section 4A-2, first paragraph. Only somatic healthcare can be given on the basis of the provisions in the chapter, and mental health without the consent of the patient must be carried out pursuant to the Mental Health Care Act, cf. PRA section 4A-2, second paragraph. Involuntary healthcare according to Chapter 4A can be implemented in various ways, and can include forced treatment, detention, restraining measures and warning system with technical devices. cf. section 4A-4. Before healthcare may be provided to which the patient objects, 'attempts must have been made to gain the patient's confidence', unless such attempts are 'obviously pointless', cf. section 4A-3. If the patient maintains his objection, or if the health personnel knows that the person concerned is very likely to maintain his objection, an administrative decision may be made regarding healthcare if:

(a) 'failure to provide healthcare may lead to significant harm to the patient's health'; and
(b) 'the healthcare is deemed to be necessary'; and
(c) 'the measures are proportionate to the need for healthcare'.

Even if the above-mentioned conditions are fulfilled, healthcare may only be provided when, after an 'overall assessment', this 'clearly appears to be the best solution for the patient', cf. section 4A-3, third paragraph. Administrative decisions regarding healthcare pursuant to Chapter 4A shall be made by the health personnel 'who are responsible for providing the healthcare', cf. section 4A-5, first paragraph. If the healthcare entails a 'serious intervention for the patient', decisions shall be made by health personnel who are responsible for providing the healthcare, after 'consultation with other qualified health personnel', cf. section 4A-5, second paragraph. In order to provide legal protection of the patients, the substantial provisions on involuntary intervention are enhanced by different forms of procedural mechanisms; cf. section 4A-6 (notification), section 4A-7 (appeals), section 4A-8 (review and subsequent monitoring), section 4A-9 (application of the PAA) and section 4A-10 (judicial review).

219. There has been one case before the Supreme Court concerning Chapter 4A. HR-2021-1263-A concerns a woman who had been subjected to compulsory health care, cf. section 4 A-5. She brought an action requesting that the last decision on compulsory healthcare be set aside. She had compound and extensive health issues largely caused and strengthened by long-term alcohol abuse. The Supreme Court found that she was not competent to consent under PRA section 4-3, and the conditions in PRA section 4A-3 were considered met. Compulsory healthcare was a necessary and proportionate measure to avoid substantial health damage, as a discharge would most likely cause her to fall back into her old drinking pattern, which might have a lethal outcome in the short run. Although she had been retained by force for three years, retention in a somatic health institution still appeared to be the best solution by far for her. The case is interesting since several legislative provisions for compulsory intervention was possible, since she had both psychiatric problems and was an alcoholic. The Supreme Court held that as long as the relevant conditions were met, and the interventions were not conflicting, different legal basis for coercive measures could be used at the same time.

220. The HPA section 7 contains provisions regarding emergency healthcare. It is built on previous regulation, but added a coercive element and broadened the duty from selected groups (physicians, dentists and midwives) to all health professionals. Health personnel 'shall immediately' provide the healthcare they are capable of when 'it must be assumed that the healthcare is of vital importance', cf. the HPA section 7, first sentence. Furthermore, pursuant to the limitations laid down by the PRA section 4-9 (*see supra* paragraph 213), 'necessary healthcare shall be given', even if the patient is 'incapable of granting his consent thereto', and even if 'the patients objects to the treatment'. The latter is clearly containing a coercive dimension, although stated in the same sentence as establishing a duty to intervene for the health personnel. In the preparatory work, the ministry emphasized that the threshold for intervention should be high, cf. also the wording 'vital importance'.[110] However, also immense pain is used as examples where intervention could be required. The ministry also included situation where the patient exposes a danger for others, although stressing that detention in psychiatric institutions can only be carried out according to the provisions in the Mental Health Act (MHA). The HPA section 7, second paragraph states that when 'in doubt' as to whether the healthcare is of vital importance, health personnel shall perform the 'necessary examinations'. This duty to provide emergency healthcare does not apply to the extent that other qualified health personnel undertakes the responsibility to provide healthcare, cf. section 7, third paragraph. Section 7 can say to be a kind of strange combination of duty of health personnel and legal basis for intrusive measures towards the patient. There are no procedural guarantees attached to intervention according to the HPA section 7, except for the general requirements (i.e., concerning documentation, etc.).

221. Rt. 2010 p. 612 concerns involuntary care for a long-term care patient (*see also supra* paragraph 68). The patient had for several years been living outside the campus of the University of Oslo and had developed difficulties with moving his arms and feet. After application, he was admitted to a nursing home and he was according to the legislation entitled to this kind of care. The patient had several wounds, which needed frequent changes of bandages, especially due to inability to control other functions. The patient objected to this care and was considered competent to give consent, in this situation to refrain from care. The legal question was whether the nursing home could change bandages and care for his wounds without the consent of the patient. The starting point for the Supreme Court was to patient's right to autonomy, expressed both in the European Convention on Human Rights (ECHR) Article 8 and PRA section 4-1. HPA section 7 did not apply since the intervention was not a case of emergency, and no other provisions could either form the

110. Ot.prp. No. 13 (1998–1999) *Om lov om helsepersonell m v (helsepersonelloven) (Regarding Act Relating to Health Personnel (The Health Personnel Act))*, 219–220.

legal basis. The majority of the Supreme Court (three judges) held that the nursing home – based on general principles of administrative law – could set as a condition that the patient underwent care of his wounds. The majority emphasized that the care was a proportionate measure and that the nursing home had tried to facilitate the implementation according to the patient's wishes. According to the majority the legal basis – based on an overall assessment – was sufficient. The minority (two judges) stressed that autonomy was a core value in health law and found that the legal basis was insufficient. The nursing home was not allowed to carry out care without the consent of the patient. The judgment is disputed, and is indeed debated among scholars.

222. The Health and Care Services Act contains in Chapter 9 provisions that opens up for coercive measures towards patients with mental disabilities. The objective of the rules in the chapter is to 'prevent people with mental disabilities from exposing themselves to serious harm and to prevent the limit the use of compulsion and power', cf. section 9-1.[111] The conditions for use of compulsion and power are stipulated in section 9-5. Intervention could only be used in the following instances (third paragraph):

(a) harm-reducing measures in emergency situations;
(b) planned harm-reducing measures in repeated emergency situations; and
(c) measures to satisfy the healthcare user or patient's fundamental needs for food and drink, clothing, rest, sleep, hygiene and personal safety, including training initiatives.

Solutions other than the use of compulsion and power must normally be tested before such measures pursuant to this chapter are initiated. cf. section 9-5, first paragraph. Compulsion and power 'may only be used when these are professionally and ethically justifiable', cf. section 9-5, second paragraph. In the assessment, 'particular emphasis must be placed on how invasive the measures are to each healthcare user or patient'. The measures 'must not exceed what is necessary for the purpose and must be in proportion to the objective that shall be ensured'. Compulsion and power 'may only be used to prevent or limit serious injury'.

223. Certain measures can only be carried out if additional requirements are fulfilled, cf. section 9-6. In order to unnecessary interventions, a set of procedural guarantees are introduced, which include full judicial review, cf. section 9-7–9-13.

111. For an in-depth analysis of the provisions in the Ch. 9, *see* Bjørn Henning Østenstad, *Heimelsspørsmål I behandling og omsorg overfor psykisk utviklingshemma og aldersdemente (Questions Regarding the Legal Basis for Treatment and Care of Mentally Disabled and Elderly with Dementia)* (Fagbokforlaget 2011).

224. The Health and Care Services Act contains in Chapter 10 provisions allowing detention of substance abusers.[112] If any person endangers his/her physical or psychological health through 'extensive and persistent substance abuse' and if assistance measures are inadequate, it can be decided that the person in question may be admitted, without his/her consent, to an institution and detained there for up to three months, cf. section 10-2. The chapter also contains a specific provision regarding pregnant women. According to section 10-3 it can be decided that a pregnant substance abuser is admitted, without her own consent, to an institution, and is detained there during the entire period of pregnancy 'if the substance abuse is such that it is highly probable that the child will be born with injury and if the assistance measures are inadequate'.

225. Patients detained pursuant by section 10-2 and 10-3 can only be held in institutions selected by the regional health authority, cf. the Specialized Health Services Act section 2-1a, fourth paragraph. Decisions according to these provisions are made by the county social welfare board, but in practice many are admitted to the institutions based by a temporary decision by the municipality, which has to be approved by the chair of the county welfare board.

§3. Privacy

226. After the revision of the Constitution in 2014, the right to privacy is now guaranteed in section 102 ('everyone has the right to respect of his private life … '). There is no single provision in the health law regulation stating the patient's right to privacy. However, the object provision in PRA states that the act should protect 'integrity and human dignity of each patient' (section 1-1), which could also include privacy elements. A recurring issue in public debate is the patient's entitlement to privacy in terms of single rooms. According to regulation of 14 November 1988 No. 932 regarding nursing home and living arrangements with twenty-four hours care and nursing section 4-1, the bedrooms should as 'a main rule' be 'single rooms'. However, twin rooms shall be available for spouses and others who want to stay together.

227. In the hospital sector, patients staying in beds at the corridors have been a repetitive concern. In 2007, a psychiatric hospital in Western Norway was imposed a coercive fine by the Norwegian Board of Health Supervision.[113] According to the supervision authorities the long-lasting placement (from 1999 and onwards) of acute psychiatric patients in the corridor of the ward was a violation of the requirements

---

112. *See* Karl Harald Søvig, *Tvang overfor rusmiddelavhengige: sosialtjenesteloven §§ 6-2 til 6-3 (Detention of Alcoholics or Drug Addicts: The Norwegian Social Services Act Sections 6-2–6-3)* (Fagbokforlaget 2007, with a summary in English). The legal basis has been amended, but the wording of the provisions is almost identical.

113. The decision is available at the website of the Norwegian Board of Health Supervision, but only in Norwegian. https://www.helsetilsynet.no/no/Publikasjoner/Brev-hoeringsuttalelser/Utvalgte-brev-og-horingsuttalelser-tidligere-ar/Tvangsmulkt-palegg-sorge-forsvarlig-helsetjeneste-Helse-Vest-RHF/?id=9139 (accessed 1 Mar. 2019).

for sufficient level of services to the patients, cf. Specialized Health Care Act section 7-2. The fine ran with a monthly amount of NOK 600,000 (approx. EUR 6,000).

§4. Secrecy

228. The PRA section 3-6 stipulates the patient's right to protection against the dissemination of information.[114] Medical and health-related information and other personal information 'shall be treated in accordance with the current provisions regarding confidentiality'. The information shall be treated with 'caution and respect for the integrity' of the person whom the information concerns. The duty of confidentiality ceases to apply to the extent that the person entitled to confidentiality so consents, cf. section 3-6, second paragraph. If health personnel disclose information that is subject to a statutory duty of disclosure, the person whom the information concerns shall, insofar as is warranted by the circumstances, be informed that the information has been given and the nature of the information in question, cf. section 3-6, third paragraph. The substantial provisions regarding medical confidentiality are stipulated in HPA Chapter 5. The rights of the patients are here mirrored by a duty of the health personnel, which at the end may be punishable.

229. According to the general rule relating to the duty of confidentiality in section 21 health personnel 'shall prevent others' from gaining access to or knowledge of information relating 'to people's health or medical condition or other personal information' that they get to know in their capacity as health personnel. The obligation is not only of passive nature (not telling), but includes also necessary active steps (security systems, etc.) in order to protect the confidentiality of patients. The case reported in Rt. 2013 p. 1422 may illustrate the obligation. An unconscious patient was brought to the hospital with narcotics in his pocket. The physician was delivering the bag with narcotics to the police for destruction, but beforehand he rubbed the bag in his hand to remove any DNA from the patient that may reveal his identity. The physician was charged for obstructing justice, but was acquitted. The Supreme Court indicates that the physician was not only entitled – but may even be obliged – to conceal the patient's identity in order to protect the confidentiality.

230. After some incidents of snooping into medical records of well-known persons, section 21a was introduced.[115] This provision clarifies that it is forbidden to 'seek, read or in any other way' to usurp, use or possess information as mentioned

114. For an in-depth analysis of the conflicting interests and the legal situation prior to the health acts of 1999, *see* Ørnulf Rasmussen, *Kommunikasjonsrett og taushetsplikt i helsevesenet (The Right to Communication and the Obligation of Confidentiality within Health Services)* (Borgund 2007).

115. Ot.prp. No. 25 (2007–2008) *Om lov om endringer i helsepersonelloven og helseregisterloven (krav til helsepersonells attester, erklæringer o.l., administrative reaksjoner og forbud mot urettmessig tilegnelse av helseopplysninger) (Regarding Act Relating to Amendments in the Health Personnel Act and the Health Register Act (Requirements for Health Personnel's Issuing of Certificates, Statements, Etc. and Prohibition of Unjust Access to Medical Information)),* 13–16 and 60–67.

in section 21 without being required due to healthcare to the patient, administration of such help or being justified by act or regulation. In HR-2018-2452-A a retired consultant physician was given a fine of NOK 15,000 (EUR 1500) for violation of HPA section 21a. Through his access to the hospital's computer system, the physician had acquired data from the claimant's medical record that he had not received from the insurance company (*see supra* paragraph 166). In HR-2021-2389-A, a healthcare worker was dismissed from her position because, without service needs, she had looked up information in a patient's medical journal. The Supreme Court of Appeal found that the dismissal met the requirements of section 15-7 subsection 1 of the Working Environment Act. The look of the information was a serious breach of duty, as it may be crucial to life and health that health personnel comply with section 21a. The conflicting relationship between the healthcare worker and the patient, and the fact that they had exchanged text messages after the offence was discovered, made the breach of trust more serious. The fact that the Norwegian Board of Health Supervision had only given the healthcare worker a warning did not prevent the employer from dismissing her. The dismissal was also not considered disproportionate.

231. The duty of confidentiality does not prevent information from being made known 'to the person that the information directly relates to, or to others', to the extent to which the person who is entitled to confidentiality gives his 'consent' thereto, cf. HPA section 22, first paragraph (*see also* PRA section 3-6, second paragraph). For persons over 16 years of age, who are incapable of considering the question of consent for reasons as mentioned in the PRA section 3-3 second paragraph, their closest next of kin may grant consent, cf. the HPA section 22, third paragraph. Particular questions may arise concerning information collected from third persons, especially within the field of psychiatry. In Rt. 1984 p. 591, a former patient claimed access to his own medical records, which also contained information provided by his former wife. He was denied access to this specific part. The Supreme Court held that the information was confidential information provided by the former wife and that no exception applied. The claim was therefore dismissed. In Rt. 2006 p. 799, a patient had given an interview shortly after surgery (preventive intervention after genetic testing). Supported by statements in the preparatory material, the Supreme Court held that it was up to the physician to prove that necessary consent existed. Since the physician could not build on the patient's consent, the patient was rewarded damages for injury of non-pecuniary character.

232. The HPA contains several exceptions of the duty of confidentiality, or clarifications, which are found in sections 22–29, and in sections 30–39. According to section 23, the duty of confidentiality pursuant to section 21 is not to prevent:

(1) information from being made known to a person who already have previous knowledge of the information;
(2) information from being provided when there are no valid interests to indicate secrecy;
(3) information from being passed on if the need for protection must be regarded as being adhered to if identifying characteristics have been omitted;

(4) information from being passed on if exceptional private or public grounds make it legitimate to pass on the information;
(5) information from being passed on when health personnel by their practice of occupation has reason to believe that animals are being exposed for such mistreatment or serious deviancy regarding environment, management and care that it is reasonable to pass on the information to the Norwegian Food Safety Authority[116] or the police; or
(6) information from being passed on in accordance with rules laid down in or pursuant to law when it has been expressly stated or clearly presumed that the duty of confidentiality shall not apply.

The exceptions stipulated in this provision are rather diverse and serve different purposes. Number 1 and 2 are based on the notion that the patient is in no need of confidentiality in these situations. Number 3 is based on the idea that the patient's identity is still being hidden. It is a practical exception, both when health personnel are sharing situations with colleagues and family, and when disseminating knowledge through medical journals. Number 4 is a general exception, based on an overall assessment of weighing the conflicting interest (for an example of such an assessment prior to the HPA, *see* Rt. 1984 p. 591). Number 5 is given in order to protect animal welfare and have several similarities with the duty to inform the children's welfare services (section 33). Number 6 is no substantial exception, but refers to other provisions and establishes a threshold ('expressly stated or clearly presumed').

233. Section 24 regulates information after a patient's death. The duty of confidentiality is not to prevent information relating to a deceased person from being passed on 'if weighty grounds so indicate'. Upon assessment of whether information shall be provided, the assumed will of the deceased, the nature of the information, as well as the interests of his next of kin and the interests of society shall be considered. The provision is prescribing a kind of overall assessment, in line with section 23 No. 4, but with a lower threshold and with more guidance of factors to be taken into consideration.

234. Sections 25 and 26 contain provisions regarding distribution of information within the healthcare system, respectively to cooperating personnel (section 25) and to the management of a facility and to administrative systems (section 26). Both provisions are based on the notion that sharing of information is necessary in order to provide the patient with healthcare of sufficient quality. Distribution of information to cooperating personnel is not to take place if the patients object thereto, cf. section 25, first paragraph. Distribution of information to the management of a facility and to administrative systems should as far as possible be given without identifying characteristics, cf. section 26, first paragraph, last sentence. Personnel receiving information pursuant to these provisions have the same obligation of confidentiality as health personnel, cf. sections 25 and 26, both last paragraphs. Separate provisions are recently introduced in order to codify existing practice.

116. This agency is also responsible for animal welfare.

According to section 25a, confidential information can be given to health personnel that works together, but this does not include access to medical records. According to section 25b, confidential information can be provided to health personnel providing actual treatment, and this even gives access to medical records. Both section 25a and section 25b state that such information cannot be given if the patients object to the information flow.

235. Disclosure of information when health personnel are acting as an expert is governed by section 27. The duty of confidentiality does not prevent health personnel acting as experts from giving information to the person or body that have assigned them as experts, 'if the information has been received in the process of carrying out this assignment and the information is significant for the assignment'. However, the provision does not regulate the information flow to the expert, but stipulates the expert's submittal of received information. According to section 27, second paragraph, anyone acting as an expert 'shall make the patient aware of the assignment and what it entails'. However, a recurring issue in many complaints brought before the Norwegian Medical Association's ethical council is stemming from lack of clarity regarding the role of physicians as experts (*see supra* paragraph 247).

236. Section 28 gives the ministry the competence to issue regulations relating to the access to pass on information relating to the medical condition of an employee to his employer to the extent that the information concerns the employee's suitability for a certain type of work or assignment. The provision is based on similar purposes as section 34 regarding information in connection with driver's licences and pilot licences. However, regulations according to section 28 are not yet given.

237. Section 29 contains provisions regarding distribution of confidential information for other purposes than in the previous sections. The alternatives regulated by section 29 are rather different (*see also* Chapter 3, §7 *infra*).Confidential information can be submitted to the purpose of statistics, quality improvement and planning. However, more information should not be provided than required, and name and identifying information may only be submitted if strictly necessary.

238. Section 29a–29d has been introduced as amendments to the HPA. Section 29a contains provisions regarding distribution concerning foreigners being transferred to compulsory mental healthcare according to the Penal Code section 62. The purpose is to provide the immigration authorities with sufficient information to make an assessment of expulsion (first paragraph) or follow-up treatment by the health authorities in the receiving state (second paragraph). Section 29b regulates the information flow for health analysis, quality improvement and administration, and is an addition to section 26. Such information can be passed on if it is of 'vital interest' of the society and if the patient's respect of 'integrity and welfare' is sufficient safeguarded. Only in 'exceptional circumstances' directly identifying information of name and personal identification number can be submitted. According to section 29c information can be passed on – based on request – from collaboration health personnel for the purpose of quality improvement or learning. However, such information can only be submitted if the patient does not object thereto. It shall be documented in the patient's medical records who has received such information and for which purpose. Section 29d regulates information to clinical ethics committee.

239. The provisions in HPA Chapter 6 establish duties of disclosure of confidential information. A common feature of all the provisions in Chapter 6 is that health personnel are obliged to pass on the information if the conditions are fulfilled. According to section 30, health personnel shall grant the supervising authority access to the 'premises of the facility' and 'provide all the information which is considered to be necessary' in order to carry out supervision of the health personnel's activities. This obligation must be seen in conjunction with the supervision authorities' task of controlling the health services, cf. *supra* paragraph 179. Notwithstanding the duty of confidentiality, the health personnel shall release the documents, sound and picture recordings, etc. required by the supervision authority, cf. section 30, last sentence.

240. Section 31 regulates information to emergency units. Health personnel shall notify the Police or the Fire Services when this is 'necessary in order to prevent serious injury or damage to person or property'. This provision is establishing a routine duty of information to these services and is based on similar purposes as section 23 No. 4.

241. Sections 32 and 33 establish notification obligations to two branches of the municipality, namely the health and care services (section 32) and to the children's welfare service (section 33). Health personnel shall in their work pay attention to matters which should lead to measures of both these services, cf. section 31, first paragraph and section 32, first paragraph. Information to social services shall be passed by own record, after having obtained the consent from the patient, or in so far as the information can be provided notwithstanding the duty of confidentiality. Additionally, both provisions established a duty for health personnel to provide information respectively to the municipal health and care services and the children's welfare services – by their own record and regardless of confidentiality – if there is 'reason to believe' that the conditions for specific involuntary interventions are fulfilled, cf. the referral to specific provision in Child Welfare Act and the Health and Care Services Act section 10-3 (pregnant substance abusers).[117] The Child Welfare Act contains a parallel regulation, which also imposes an obligation for health personnel, cf. section 6-4.

242. According to HPA section 34, physicians, psychologists or optometrists who find that a patient holding a driver's licence for motor vehicles or a pilot licence for aircraft does not fulfil the necessary medical requirements shall inform the

117. For a presentation of the latter, *see* Karl Harald Søvig, *Detention of Pregnant Women to Protect the Foetus*, in *Nordic Health Law in a European Context* 158–180 (Elisabeth Rynning & Mette Hartlev eds, Liber/Brill 2011).

patient that it is prohibited to drive or fly. Previously, the obligation was to encourage the patient to hand in his/her license. If the patient's medical condition is 'presumed not to be of a temporal nature', the health personnel as mentioned, 'shall report' this to the public authorities in accordance with further provisions laid down by the ministry in regulations. Such provisions are given by Regulation of 4 March 2022 No. 325.

243. While the duties in HPA Chapter 6 is based on an assessment of individual cases the notification requirements in the HPA Chapter 7 is more on a systematic level, although some of the provision require an individual assessment. According to section 35, physicians and midwives shall notify the National Population Register of births. The notification shall also include the name of the father or whom the mother has named as the father. The purpose of this duty is to secure up-to-date and accurate population registers. Additionally, physicians and midwives shall give notification to deliveries and termination of pregnancies following the twelfth week to the Medical Birth Registry, cf. section 35, fourth paragraph. The Medical Birth Registry was established in 1967 and contains information of all births since then, and provides a basis for epidemiological research with a large data set.

244. According to section 36, physicians shall provide notifications of deaths. This provision is also based on a dual purpose, partly to secure up-to-date and accurate population registers and partly to provide basis for research. If there is reason to suspect that a person 'did not die of natural causes', the physician shall report to the police, cf. section 36, third paragraph. The object is here to unravel the death cause. Additionally, if investigations have been instigated in order to determine if 'death occurred by a criminal offence', the physician shall provide the court with information that is relevant to the case provided the court requests it.

245. Section 37 stipulates the duty of health personnel to provide information health personnel holding an authorization or licence to provide information to personal health data filing systems in accordance with regulations laid down pursuant to the Health Register Act. This act gives, *inter alia,* the ministry the competence to establish registers containing information provided without the consent of the patient, based on prior decision by the parliament, cf. section 8. The establishment of such registers and the procedural requirements has been much disputed in Norway.

246. The duty of confidentiality according to the HPA section 21 applies to all health personnel, in addition to their helpers, cf. section 25, third paragraph. A separate system for duty of confidentiality is established by PAA. This duty applies to all civil servants and others carrying out tasks for the authorities. Health personnel working for public entities will therefore have a dual duty of confidentiality, cf. Specialized Health Care Act section 6-1 reiterating this duty and also imposing some additional regulations to the PAA. In cases of dual duty of confidentiality, the most strict will have supremacy, which without exceptions will be the rules deriving from the HPA.

§5. COMPLAINTS

247. PRA Chapter 7 contains different forms of procedural remedies of the patient, while review by the Patient Ombudsperson is established by Chapter 8. PRA distinguishes between complaints (section 7-2) and request for assessment of possible breach of duty (section 7-4). According to section 7-2, a patient – or a representative of the patient – can complain of a violation of the provisions in Chapter 2 (The right to healthcare and transport), Chapter 3 (The right to participation and information), Chapter 4 (Consent to healthcare), section 5-1 (Right to access to medical records), section 6-2 (Children's right to be accompanied by their parents while staying in a health institution) and section 6-3 (Children's right to activity while staying in a health institution). The complaint body is the county governor. Complaints regarding breach of section 241a, second paragraph litra a (entitlement of the patient to necessary healthcare outside the country if there is no offer in Norway or the health care abroad is documented to be more effective than the health care offered by the public sector in Norway) are reviewed by a board appointed by the ministry, cf. section 7-2, second paragraph. The provision in section 7-2, first paragraph applies simultaneously to persons who have an individual entitlement according to Chapters 3–6, cf. section 7-2, fifth paragraph. This could, for example, be persons of next of kin having an individual right to information. The complaints mechanisms must also be viewed in connection with supervision instruments, *see supra* paragraph 177.

248. The complaint shall be in writing and signed by the patient or the person having an individual right, or their representative, *cf.* section 7-3. The complaint should state the 'matter that is the subject of the complaint' and 'provide information that may be of significance' for consideration of the complaint. If the complaint contains 'errors or deficiencies', the county governor shall set a brief time limit for rectification or supplementation. These provisions are copied from the PAA section 32, cf. the PRA section 7-6 regarding the application of the PAA. The time limit for complaints is four weeks, cf. section 7-5 (deviates from the time limit of three weeks in the PAA).

249. The patient or other persons who are entitled to do so may, if they are of the opinion that provisions concerning duties laid down in or pursuant to the HPA, the Specialized Health Care Act, the Health and Care Services Act or the Dental Health Services Act have been 'breached in his or her disfavour', request the supervisory authority to consider the matter, cf. section 7-4. The same entitlement is vested to the closest next of kin of a diseased patient and for the closest next of kin of a patient over 18 years without the competence to consent. These provisions address relevant acts besides the PRA, where the patient – except for the Dental Health Services – is not given individual rights and would therefore not be considered as having a standing as applicant.

250. Section 7-4, second paragraph reiterates the remedies of the supervision bodies. They may, if appropriate, impose an administrative sanction pursuant to Chapter 11 of the HPA, request for public prosecution pursuant to the HPA section

67 and impose orders to healthcare providers according to the Health Supervision Act section 5 and the Specialized Health Care Act section 7-1. Procedural requirements for the request for assessment of possible breach of duty are stipulated in section 7-4a.

251. The relationship between the general procedural requirements in the PAA and the specific procedural requirements of the PRA is complicated and regulated by PRA section 7-7. On the one hand, the general provisions are meant also to regulate the special branches of the administration. On the other hand, provision of healthcare has its particularities, where the procedures established in the PAA can be too firm. However, the object of protecting the patient's rights calls for a thorough procedure. The balancing of the competing interests has led to the adaption of the PAA in the PRA section 7-7, which has been amended several times since the introduction of PRA.

252. The Patient's Ombudsperson shall work to meet patients' needs and protect their interests and legal rights in respect of the health service (both primary and specialist level), and to improve the quality of the health service, cf. PRA section 8-1. The government shall ensure that there is a Patient's Ombudsperson in every county, cf. section 8-2, first paragraph. The Patient's Ombudsperson shall perform his or her functions independently and autonomously, cf. section 8-2, third paragraph. The Patient's Ombudsperson may take up for consideration cases concerning matters in the public health service, either on the basis of an oral or written request or on his or her own initiative, cf. section 8-3, first paragraph. Any person may contact the Patient's Ombudsperson and request that a case be taken up for consideration, cf. section 8-3, second paragraph. The person who contacts the Patient's Ombudsperson is entitled to be anonymous. The Patient's Ombudsperson himself or herself shall decide whether a request gives 'sufficient grounds' for taking a case up for consideration. If the Patient's Ombudsperson does not take the case up for consideration, the person who made the request shall be notified and given a brief explanation for this decision. In order to have sufficient basis for the decision, the Patient's Ombudsperson is entitled to receive information (section 8-5) and has access to health service premises (section 8-6). The responsibilities are stipulated in section 8-7. The Patient's Ombudsperson shall, to a reasonable extent, give anyone who makes a request to information, advice and guidance in matters that lay within the Patient's Ombudsperson's sphere of responsibility, cf. section 8-7, first paragraph. The Patient's Ombudsperson is entitled to state his or her opinion on matters that lie within the Ombudsperson's sphere of responsibility, and to propose specific measures for improvement, cf. section 8-7, third paragraph. The statements are 'not binding'. The system of the Patient's Ombudsman is therefore based on the authority and the persuasion of the decision, and not the formal basis.

§6. Access to Medical Records

253. The patient's access to medical records was established by the Supreme Court in the decision reported in Rt. 1977 p. 1035. A former patient requested to have access to his medical records after a hospital stay. The request was not connected to a lawsuit, where the patient according to established principles could be entitled to documents possessed by the opposite party. The hospital claimed that the medical record was an internal document, which also was owned by the physician. The Supreme Court held that neither the rules in the PAA or the Freedom of Information Act was applicable. However, after an assessment of the conflicting interests the Supreme Court came to the conclusion that the patient was entitled to access his own medical records based on common legal principles. The access to medical records was then written into the 1980 Act relating to rights and duties of medical doctors and dentists. The General Data Protection Regulation (2016/679) also applies to Norway according to the EEA Agreement (*see* the Personal Data Act, 15 June 2018 No. 38).

254. While the regulation of medical confidentiality is found in the HPA, the patient's right to access to medical records is stipulated by the PRA Chapter 5, cf. also the referral in the HPA section 41. Provisions regarding the content of the medical record and the duties of health personnel in this respect are found in the HPA Chapter 7. The patient is according to section 5-1, first paragraph 'entitled' to have access to his or her medical records with enclosures and may have a copy. Upon request, the patient is entitled to a 'brief and simple explanation' of medical terms, etc. The patient may be denied access to information in his or her medical records if this is 'absolutely necessary' in order to avoid endangering the patient's life or serious damage to the patient's health, or if access is clearly inadvisable out of consideration for persons close to the patient, cf. section 5-1, second paragraph. In such cases, a representative of the patient is entitled to have access to the information to which the patient is denied access, unless the representative is considered to be unfit for this, cf. section 5-1, third paragraph. A 'physician or lawyer' may not be denied access, unless special reasons so dictate. The next of kin are entitled to have access to medical records after a patient's death, unless special reasons dictate otherwise, cf. section 5-1, fifth paragraph and the HPA section 24, second paragraph.

255. Further rules regarding medical records are given by regulation of 1 March 2019 No. 168. Besides addressing access issues, the regulation also contains provisions regarding the content of medical records, cf. also HPA Chapter 8. According to section 11, health personnel shall facilitate for access patients speaking Sami or foreign languages, as well as patients with impairments. Access to medical records should as a main rule be free of charge, but a fee could apply if the patients request multiply copies, with reference to the General Data Protection Regulation Article 15 No. 3.

256. Section 5-2 regulates correction and erasure of medical records. The patient or the 'person whom the information concerns' may demand that the information in the medical records be corrected or erased pursuant to the provisions of the HPA sections 42 to 44. Provisions regarding transfer and loan of medical records are found in section 5-3. The patient is 'entitled to object' to the disclosure of his or her medical records or information in the records. Furthermore, the information may not be disclosed if there is 'reason to believe' that the patient would have objected to this if asked. The information may nonetheless be disclosed if 'weighty grounds' so dictate.

Chapter 2. The Physician-Patient Relationship in Specific Terms

§1. The Minor Patient

257. The starting point is that the minor patient has the same entitlements as adults. However, some specific provisions are necessary in order to provide a sufficient legal protection of minor patients.[118] It should also be kept in mind that the minor patient covers a large age gap, from infants to persons just below the age of 18 years, with large differences between the individuals at the same age. The general age of majority in Norway is 18 years, cf. the Guardianship Act section 8. The PRA has a separate chapter stipulating 'special rights for children', cf. Chapter 6. Additionally, several of the other provisions in the PRA and in other parts of the legislation have specific rules concerning children. A guiding principle for all decision concerning children, i.e., both when in interpretation of the legislation and when making decisions on behalf of children, is that the best interest of the child should be a primary consideration, anchored both in the Constitution (section 104), binding international human right's instruments (UN Convention on the Rights of the Child, section 3) and various national legislation (like the Children Act section 30).

258. According to the PRA section 4-3, first paragraph, litra b) patients between 16 and 18 years of age are entitled to give consent, unless 'special provisions' or the 'nature of the measure' dictate otherwise. The age of majority within health law will therefore be 16 years of age, but with exceptions. They could either be stipulated in the legislation, or based on the 'nature of the measure'. It was, for example, a common understanding among legal scholars and by health authorities that children under the age of 18 cannot undergo cosmetic surgery which is not necessary for medical purposes.[119] Still, the legislator wanted to clarify the situation and introduced section 4-5a. According to this provision, persons under the age of 18 years cannot consent to cosmetic interventions, injections or treatment that does not have a medical or odontological purpose. Neither can parents nor holders of parental responsibility give such a consent. On the other hand, also before the age of 16 patients could be competent to give a consent on their own behalf, i.e., regarding contraception, cf. *infra*. The provisions in the PRA applies to a large extent simultaneously also in other situations. An illustrative example is consent to in cases of medical confidentiality, where the HPA section 22, second paragraph refers to the PRA section 4-4 (consent) and section 3-4 (information).

118. *See* Henriette Sinding Aasen, *Barns rett til selvbestemmelse og medbestemmelse i beslutninger om helsehjelp (Children's Right to Self-Determination and Cooperation in Decisions Regarding Health Care),* 6(1) Tidsskrift for familierett, arverett og barnevernrettslige spørsmål (J. Fam. L., Inheritance L. & Child Protec. Leg. Issues) 4–27 (2008).

119. Cf. Aslak Syse, *Pasient- og brukerrettighetsloven med kommentarer (The Patient- and User Rights Act – A Commentary)* 412 (4th ed., Gyldendal 2015).

259. Section 4-4 regulates consent on behalf of children which are not competent to give their own consent. The parents or other persons with parental responsibility are entitled to consent to healthcare for patients under 16 years of age, cf. section 4-4, first paragraph. According to section 4-4, second paragraph it is sufficient with the consent of one of the parents or holder of the parental responsibility for treatment being considered as part of the daily and ordinary care for the child (litra a) with reference to the Children Act section 37 and section 42, second paragraph). This also applies to parents without parental responsibility, except in cases of vaccination according to the ordinary programme for childhood vaccination. Section 4-4 third paragraph addresses situations where qualified health personnel finds that healthcare is necessary to prevent the child from harm. Then consent from one of the parents or holders of parental responsibility is sufficient. Section 4-4, third paragraph is practical for parents not living together, and the provision also contains procedural requirements. Before such healthcare is carried out, the other parent should as far as possible be heard. The decision can be appealed to the county governor, which can decide to postpone the care until a decision upon the appeal is reached. If the child welfare service has taken a child under 16 years of age into care pursuant to section 4-8 or section 4-12 of the Child Welfare Act, the child welfare service has the right to consent to healthcare, cf. section 4-4, fourth paragraph.

260. In 2017, amendments were introduced in order to strengthen the position of children concerning health and care services partly due to criticism from the UN Committee on the Rights of the child (amendment 16 June 2017 No. 53).[120] Children who are able of making their own viewpoints shall be given information and shall be heard, cf. section 3-1 first paragraph. The legal entitlement for minors to receive information and to be involved were explicitly regulated, cf. section 3-4. Children between the age of 12 and 16 years old were entitled in some situation to consent on their own, cf. section 4-3 first paragraph litra c. Health personnel were entitled to make decision regarding healthcare for minors under the age of 12 years old which is strictly necessary and not of intrusive character if the requirements for not sharing information according to section 3-4 third paragraph are fulfilled, cf. PRA section 4-3 sixth paragraph. Such a decision is only to be made for a limited period until a consent can be given.[121]

261. Consent on behalf of young people who are not competent to give consent is regulated by section 4-5, i.e., children with physical or mental impairment making them unable to consent, or in cases according to section 4-3, first paragraph litra b) where a child is not considered competent to consent. Parents or other persons with parental responsibility have the right to consent to healthcare for patients between 16 and 18 years of age who are not competent to give consent, cf. section 4-5, first paragraph. If the child welfare service has taken a child between 16 and 18

---

120. Cf. CRC/C/NOR/CO/4 (2010), para. 24.

121. Prop.75 L (2016–2017) *Endringar i pasient- og brukarrettslova, helsepersonellova m.m. (styrking av rettsstillinga til barn ved yting av helse- og omsorgstenester m.m) (Amendments in the Patient's and Care Act, the Health Personnel Act, Etc. (Improvement of the Legal Position of Children in Regards to Health and Care Services)).*

years of age into care pursuant to section 4-8 or section 4-12 of the Child Welfare Act, the child welfare service has the right to consent to healthcare, cf. section 4-5, second paragraph. Healthcare 'may not be provided if the patient objects thereto', unless special statutory provisions dictate otherwise, cf. section 4-5, third paragraph. If the patient objects, healthcare may be given in accordance with the provisions in the PRA section 4A.

262. Situations can occur where the parents wish to continue treatment of children, while health personnel finds that continued treatment is not in the best interest of the child. Especially cases concerning infants have arisen in practice, typically where the child is severely injured. Cases have been for the courts, but none of them has reached the Supreme Court. The system of the PRA addresses situations where a consent is needed and does not have a specific regulation of termination of treatment.[122]

263. As with adults, the ability to consent is closely linked to information. The information flow when the patient is a minor is regulated by the PRA section 3-4, which was reformed during the above-mentioned reform in 2017. If the patient is under 16 years of age, both 'the patient and his or her parents or other persons with parental responsibility' shall be informed, cf. section 3-4, first paragraph. If the patient is between 12 and 16 years of age, information shall not be given to his or her parents or other persons with parental responsibility when the patient, for reasons that should be respected, does not wish them to receive such information, cf. section 3-4, second paragraph. As examples for legitimate reasons the ministry uses in the preparatory work both maltreatment and bullying.[123] This provision provides the health personnel with a professional leeway, where they have to take into consideration both the child's need for privacy towards their parents and the parents need of information about their children. Regardless of age, information should not be passed on to the parents or care holders if compelling reasons are against it, cf. section 3-4, third paragraph. However, information that is 'necessary to fulfil parental responsibility' shall be given to parents or other persons with parental responsibility when the patient is under 18 years of age, cf. section 3-4, fourth paragraph. In the preparatory work, the ministry uses as examples suicide risk, the whereabouts of the patient and life-threatening conditions. If the child welfare service has taken a child under 16 years of age into care pursuant to section 4-8 or section 4-12 of the Child Welfare Act, the first, second and third paragraphs shall apply correspondingly to the child welfare service, cf. section 3-4, sixth paragraph.

264. The remedies of intervention according to the Child Welfare Act will not be dealt with here, but two provisions are of special interest for health law purposes. According to section 4-10, the county board for child welfare and social

122. Karl Harald Søvig, "Reviewing Medical Decisions Concerning Infants within the Norwegian Healthcare System: A Public Law Approach", in *Medical Decision-Making on Behalf of Young Children: A Comparative Perspective*, Imogen Goold et al (eds.), Hart Publishing 2020, 259-268

123. Ot.prp. No. 12 (1998–1999) *Lov om pasientrettigheter (pasientrettighetsloven) (Act Relating to Patient's Right),* 131.

affairs can issue orders for medical examination and treatment. If there is 'reason to believe' that a child is suffering from a 'life-threatening or other serious illness or injury', and if the parents fail to ensure that the child is examined or receives treatment, the county board may decide that the child with the assistance of the child welfare service shall be examined by a doctor, or be taken to a hospital for examination. The county board may also decide that such an illness shall be treated at a hospital or at home in accordance with a doctor's instructions. Section 4-11 provides the county board with the competence to issue treatment orders for children with special treatment and training needs. Such an order may be issued if the parents fail to 'ensure that a child who is disabled or in special need of help receives the treatment and training required'. The county board may then decide that the child shall receive treatment or training with the assistance of the child welfare service. Orders according to section 4-10 and section 4-11 are in practice seldom issued, but some cases have gained much media attention.

265. As mentioned previously, the PRA contains special provision for children in Chapter 6 which will be presented in the following text. According to section 6-1 children are entitled to necessary healthcare, also in the form of health checks in the municipality in which the child lives or is staying temporarily, cf. the Health and Care Service Act section 3-2. Parents are 'obliged' to contribute to the health check of their children, cf. section 6-1, second paragraph.

266. Section 6-2–6-4 regulates children's rights during stay in health institutions. Such provisions came into the regulation as a response to previous practices, where children could be hospitalized for long periods without contact with their parents (prior to the PRA similar provisions were found in regulations according to the Hospital Act). According to section 6-2, Children are 'entitled to be accompanied' by at least one parent or other person with parental responsibility during their entire stay in a health institution, unless this is inadvisable out of consideration for the child, or the right of contact has ceased to apply pursuant to the provisions of the Children Act or the Child Welfare Act. Furthermore, children are 'entitled to be kept active and stimulated' during their stay in a health institution to the extent that this is justifiable in the light of the child's health condition, cf. section 6-3. Children and adolescents are 'entitled to tuition' while staying in a health institution to the extent that this is in accordance with the Education Act, cf. section 6-4, first and second paragraph. Pre-school children are entitled to special educational assistance while staying in a health institution to the extent that this is in accordance with the Education Act, cf. section 6-4, third paragraph. Also the Specialized Health Care Act contains specific provision regarding children in hospitals or other specialized institutions. According to section 3-6, the ministry can by regulation stipulate further requirements concerning both, the facilities at the institutions and reimbursement of the extra costs of for the parents (transport, etc.). Such provisions are given by regulation (1 December 2000 No. 1217). The regulation states, *inter alia*, that children should normally be admitted in separate units (section 4). Departments that regularly receive children should have separate parts for children. Children shall not be placed in rooms together with adults that have a condition which could frighten the child.

267. The legislation also contains some provisions regulating issues arising when the child's parents are in institutions. These provisions are recently introduced as recognition of children as next of kin are in a vulnerable situation and in order to strengthen their legal protection.[124] Health personnel shall take care of the need for information and follow-up of children of patients with psychiatric diseases, substance addiction or severe somatic illnesses injury, cf. the HPA section 10a, which were revised during the amendments in 2017 (16 June 2017 No. 53). The provision also contains examples of different measures that can be used in order to support the child's need. According to the HPA section 25, third paragraph confidential information may be submitted to cooperating health personnel when this is necessary in order to protect the interests of the patient's children. According to the Specialized Health Care Act section 3-7a, institution should, if necessary, have special qualified personnel with the responsibility to promote and coordinate health personnel's follow-up of minor children of patients with mental health problems, addiction or somatic patients with a serious condition. Health personnel shall take care of the need for information and follow-up of children of children who have lost their parents or siblings, cf. the HPA section 10b.

§2. The Mental Patient

268. The legal protection of mental patients in Norway has undergone a shift, where this patient group originally was considered to be in need of special regulation. There has then been a development towards inclusion, thus providing mental patients with the same entitlements as other patients. The legal protection of mental patients is also a contemporary debate, where some voices claim that every special regulation of mental patients are discriminatory, and also a breach of the UN Convention on the Rights of Persons with Disabilities.[125]

269. The Mental Health Care Act was one of the four legal siblings of the major 1999 health law reform. It replaced the MHA from 1961, which in turn replaced the first MHA from 1848. The Mental Health Care Act was followed up by several regulations addressing different specific issues. After a reform in 2011, the ministry issued a single regulation in order to have a more transparent legislation (16 December 2011 No. 1258). A major reform was made in 2017 in order to improve the right to self-determination and protect the rule of law (amendment 10 February 2017 No. 6). The Mental Health Care Act Chapter 1 contains definitions and clarification of

124. *See* the elaboration of the purposes in Ot.prp. No. 84 (2008–2009*) Om lov om endringar i helsepersonelloven m.m. (oppfølging av born som pårørande) (Regarding Act Relating to Amendments in the Health Personnel Act, Etc. (Follow Up of Children as Next of Kin)).*

125. *See* NOU 2011:9 *Økt selvbestemmelse og rettssikkerhet – Balansegangen mellom selvbestemmelsesrett og omsorgsansvar i psykisk helsevern (Increased self-Determination and Legal Protection – The Balancing between Autonomy and Care Responsibility in Psychiatric Care)* and NOU 2019: 14 *Tvangsbegrensningsloven – Forslag til felles regler om tvang og inngrep uten samtykke i helse- og omsorgstjenesten (Act regarding limitation of coercion – Draft for common legislation for coercion and intervention without consent in health and care services).*In both reports, the minority have a dissenting opinion.

the interplay with other parts of the legislation. Chapter 2 contains special provisions regarding consent. Chapter 3 contains provisions regarding application and termination of compulsory mental healthcare. Chapter 4 contains provisions regarding implementation of mental healthcare. Chapter 4A was introduced as a response for a call for units with a higher security level, which also includes more intrusive measures towards the patients (amendment 22 June 2012 No. 48).[126] Chapter 5 contains provisions regarding court order for transfer to compulsory mental healthcare, which is a criminal sanction and will not be dealt with here. Chapter 6 contains provisions on supervision and review, while Chapter 7 regulates judicial review.

270. The legal starting point is equal treatment of patients regardless of their diagnosis. The PRA applies therefore also for psychiatric patients. However, this is a more recent approach. Until 2006 (amendment 30 June 2006 No. 45), the Mental Health Care Act section 1-5 stated that the PRA only applied for psychiatric patients insofar it was 'appropriate'. It now applies directly, although with some adjustments. At the primary level, there are few special provisions regarding psychiatric patients. However, at the secondary level the Mental Health Care Act is a central legal tool. According to section 1-2, first paragraph the term 'mental healthcare' shall mean the examination and treatment by 'specialized health services of persons suffering from mental illness', and the nursing and care that this requires. The object of the Act is to ensure that mental healthcare is 'applied and implemented in a satisfactory manner and in accordance with the fundamental principles of the rule of law', cf. section 1-1. The provision continues to add as object 'to ensure that the measures described in the Act are grounded on the needs of the patient and respect for human dignity'.

271. A recurrent discussion has been which education and background that is necessary for taking decision within this field, especially regarding coercive elements. The mental health professional responsible for making administrative decisions and for deciding on more closely specified measures pursuant to this Act shall be a 'physician with relevant specialist approval' or 'clinical psychologist with relevant practice and supplementary education' as laid down in regulations, cf. section 1-4. However, the use of medicine must be decided by a physician, cf. regulation of 16 December 2011 No. 1258 section 27, first paragraph.

272. The general rule regarding consent is that mental healthcare 'is provided on the basis of consent' pursuant to the provisions in the PRA, unless otherwise provided for in the Mental Health Care Act, cf. section 2-1. A special provision is given for children, cf. section 2-1, second paragraph. In the case of examination or treatment with a stay in an institution for children who are over the age of 12 and 'who do not themselves agree with the measure', the question of applying mental healthcare shall be brought before the supervisory commission. This provision guarantees an independent assessment in such cases where in order to protect the child's best

126. Prop.108 L (2011–2012) *Endringer i psykisk helsevernloven (regionale sikkerhetsavdelinger og enhet med særlig høyt sikkerhetsnivå m.m.) (Amendments to the Mental Health Care Act (Regional Security Wards and Unit with Special High Security Level, Etc.)).*

interest. Examination and treatment of patients with a mental disorder who lack competence to consent and is suspected to have a serious mental disorder or opposes the healthcare, can only be made pursuant to the provisions regarding compulsory care in Mental Health Care Act Chapter 3, cf. PRA section 4-3, fifth paragraph. This provision is made in order to protect the legal position of mental patients. The same purpose is the rational of PRA section 4A-2, second paragraph. According to this provision mental healthcare cannot be given pursuant to Chapter 4A (healthcare for patients without competence to give consent who object to healthcare).

273. A rather peculiar provision is found in section 2-2. The patient may consent to being subject to the rules regarding compulsory mental healthcare (Ulyssean coercion). Any person who seeks mental healthcare may, at the 'request of the responsible mental health professional', consent to be subject to the rules pursuant to section 3-5 for up to three weeks from the date the care is provided. The period is limited, but within this frame the patient can be placed in a locked ward. The provision is useful with patient with an ambivalent attitude, for example, substance abusers. The patient uses, in these cases, his own autonomy to restrict his or hers freedom of liberty for a limited time. Such consent does not entail consent to application of section 4-4 (treatment without the consent) or section 4-5, second paragraph (restrict to receive visits and use the telephone). Procedural requirements are laid down in section 2-2, third paragraph, and the core element in the written agreement between the responsible healthcare professional and the patient. This document is partly a consent (from the patient) and partly an administrative decision (from the hospital). This provision also contains a rule of substantial character. In the case of persons who 'owing to physical or mental disorders, senile dementia or learning disabilities are clearly not able to understand what consent entails', the responsible mental health professional and any person acting on behalf of the patient, shall sign the document, subject to the limitations following from PRA section 4-3. This provision opens up for represented consent in a rather problematic way, since the purpose of the section is the patient's acknowledgment of his own disease. Agreements according to section 2-2 may also be entered into by children, or by their parents. As with ordinary voluntary care, disagreement between children over the age of 12 and their children leave the decision to the supervisory commission, cf. section 2-2, fifth paragraph.

274. Temporary detention can be made pursuant to section 3-2 (ten days with the possibility of one renewal). The conditions in section 3-2 are almost the same as in section 3-3, which opens up for detention of an indefinite time. On the basis of information from the medical examination pursuant to section 3-1 and compulsory observation, if any, pursuant to section 3-2, the responsible mental health professional shall assess whether the conditions for compulsory mental healthcare are satisfied. These are formulated as follows:

(1) Voluntary mental healthcare has been tried, to no avail, or it is obviously pointless to try this.
(2) The patient has been examined by two physicians, one of whom shall be independent of the responsible institution, cf. section 3-1.

(3) The patient is suffering from a serious mental disorder and application of compulsory mental healthcare is necessary to prevent the person concerned from either:
   (a) having the prospects of his or her health being restored or significantly improved considerably reduced, or it is highly probable that the condition of the person concerned will significantly deteriorate in the very near future, or
   (b) constituting an obvious and serious risk to his or her own life and health or those of others on account of his or her mental disorder.
(4) The patient lacks the competence to consent. This requirement does not apply if the patient constitutes an obvious and serious risk to his or others life (No. 4 was introduced as part of the reform in 2017).
(5) The institution is professionally and materially capable of offering the patient satisfactory treatment and care and is approved in accordance with section 3-5.
(6) The patient has been given the opportunity to state his or her opinion, cf. section 3- 9.
(7) Even though the conditions of the Act are otherwise satisfied, compulsory mental healthcare may only be applied when, after an overall assessment, this clearly appears to be the best solution for the person concerned, unless he or she constitutes an obvious and serious risk to the life or health of others. When making the assessment, special emphasis shall be placed on how great a strain the compulsory intervention will entail for the person concerned.

275. The Norwegian Supreme Court is from time to time reviewing cases concerning decisions according to section 3-3 (the courts have in such cases competence to a full review, cf. paragraph 324 *infra*). Some cases have concerned the basic requirement ('serious mental disorder'), cf. Rt. 2015 p. 913. A female patient with anorexia nervosa was detained (with the aim of forced feeding, cf. section 4-4, second paragraph, litra b). The court appointed experts held that her anorexia was of grave character and was equivalent with a psychosis. The Supreme Court found that her condition represented a serious mental disorder. In recent years, a recurrent issue has been the additional condition in section 3-3, No. 3, litra a, second alternative in situation where the patient is likely to stop taking medicine after release. In Rt. 2014 p. 801, the Supreme Court held that a relapse within three to four months fell within the term 'very near future'. This approach represented an adjustment compared to previous case law and the guidance given in the preparatory work. The Supreme Court emphasized that the assessment must be made on basis of the duration of effect of modern psycho pharmaceutics. HR-2016-1286-A concerns a woman who was taken under compulsory mental healthcare pursuant to HRA section 3-3, who was receiving treatment involving first generation depot anti-psychotics. An argument that compulsory treatment of mentally ill patients based on informed consent, on its own is a breach of human rights, if this happens solely in the interests of their own health, did not succeed. The Supreme Court also concluded that the expression 'in the near future' in section 3-3, subsection 1 no. 3, litra a) – 'the deterioration option' – must be interpreted in the same way as for patients who are treated with first generation depot anti-psychotics, as for patients treated with second generation anti-psychotics, i.e., a time frame of three to four months, cf. Rt-2014-801. There were then still grounds for compulsory mental healthcare. HR-2018-2204-A concerns a woman who had been under forced mental healthcare for almost seven years under MHA section 3-3, due to a schizoaffective disorder, a mixed manic-depressive type. During the last five years, the force had consisted of attendance every four weeks for depot medication. The Supreme Court found that the woman had no real insight into her own situation and did not understand the consequences of terminating the treatment. The requirement regarding competence to give consent was thus met, *see* PRA section 4-3 subsection 2. It was also highly likely that her condition would become worse by seponating the medicine, although it was doubtful that the deterioration would occur within three to four months after the discharge, as the Act requires. Following an overall assessment under MHA section 3-3, seventh paragraph, the Supreme Court found, with considerable doubt, that the discharge request had to be complied with. Emphasis was placed on the treatment for nearly five years being limited to maintenance, on the doubt related to the time aspect of the deterioration requirement and on the legislature's stressing of patients' self-determination. In HR-2020-1167-A, a patient suffering from serious eating disorders had demanded lifting of compulsory mental healthcare. It was not disputed that the requirements of serious mental illness, of deterioration and of risk in section 3-3 of the Compulsory Mental Health Care Act were met. The Supreme Court also found that the exception in section 3-3 (4) second sentence from the requirement of inability to give consent was met. It was assumed that the exception is not limited to apply to risk of suicide, but that it also comprises cases where the patient's life is in acute danger without this being connected to the risk of suicide. The condition in (4) was thus considered met. In the overall assessment under section 3-3 (7), compulsory mental healthcare appeared to be the best solution. The request for lifting was dismissed.

276. The implementation rules of mental healthcare is as a starting point the same, regardless of the legal status of the patient (admitted with consent or compulsory care), cf. Chapter 5. However, voluntarily admitted patient may at any time withdraw the consent. Additionally, some of the provisions apply only to patients admitted in accordance with section 3-3, for example, involuntary treatment (section 4-4) and restriction on visits and use of telephone (section 4-5, second paragraph).

277. While other patients group have the county governor as their main supervision body, patients under mental healthcare can address their complaints to the supervisory commission. Rules concerning the procedure and composition of the commission are found in Chapter 6. The supervisory commission is appointed by the ministry, but is 'autonomous in its activity', cf. section 6-3, first paragraph. The commission shall review all decisions regarding involuntary admittance (section 3-2 and section 3-3), cf. section 3-8. The commission shall 'assure itself that the correct procedure has been followed and that the administrative decision is based on an assessment of the conditions'. If the application of compulsory mental healthcare is not appealed, the supervisory commission shall nevertheless, three months after the decision was made, on 'its own initiative' assess whether there is a need for compulsory care and make sure that an individual plan has been drawn up for the patient, cf. 3-8, second paragraph. The commission can either take up cases by their own motion or based on complaints from patients, their next of kin or personnel at the institution, cf. section 6-1, second paragraph. The patient can, for example, appeal the decision regarding detention to the supervisory commission, which is competent to make a full review of the case. Certain decisions are not within the competence of the commission, like forced treatment according to section 4-4. The complaint body is in such cases the county governor, based in their expertise in medical issues. According to the 2017 amendments to the MHA, patients complaining over forced treatment are now granted free legal aid (cf. Act relating to free legal aid section 11, first paragraph No. 8).

278. Administrative decisions of the supervisory commission in cases concerning compulsory observation, the application or the maintenance of compulsory mental healthcare pursuant to section 3-2, 3-3 and 3-7 'may be brought before the court by the patient or his or her next-of-kin' pursuant to the provisions of the Civil Procedure Act Chapter 36 (the same applies to decisions according to sections 4-10 and 5-4.), cf. section 7-1. Chapter 36 contains special provision in cases concerning decisions on coercive measures in the health and social services. Such cases shall be given priority and the court can review all aspects of the case.

§3. The Dying Patient

279. There are some provisions directly addressing issues regarding a dying patient. As mentioned earlier (*see supra* paragraph 167), assisted suicide is not allowed. A dying patient could therefore not request a physician of a lethal dose of morphine or similar drugs. However, as pointed out by the ethical council of the Norwegian Medical Association, there are several grey areas and there is an ongoing public debate (*see supra* paragraph 192). This is partly fertilized by media coverage of dying patient travelling to countries with a more liberal approach.[127]

280. A provision directly addressing the legal situation of dying patients is PRA section 4-9, second paragraph (for a presentation of other parts of the provision, *see* paragraph 214). According to this provision a 'dying patient' is 'entitled to object to life-prolonging treatment'. If a dying patient is incapable of communicating his or her wishes as regards treatment, the health personnel shall refrain from providing healthcare if the patient's next of kin express similar wishes, and the health personnel, based on an independent assessment, find that this is also the patient's wish and that the wish should clearly be respected.

127. For an in-depth analysis of the legal situation before the PRA, which is still of relevance, *see* Erling Johannes Husabø, *Rett til sjølvvalt livsavslutning? (A Right to Voluntary End of Life?)* 557–568 (Gyldendal 1994, with summary and conclusions in English).

Chapter 3. Specific Activities

§1. Abortion

281. Rules concerning abortion are found in the Abortion Act.[128] The Act was enacted in 1975. The women's right to self-determination was introduced in 1978 by an amendment to the act (16 June 1978 No. 66), after a divided political process. According to section 1, the society shall, 'as far as possible', ensure all children the necessary conditions for a secure childhood and adolescence. As part of this work, the society shall ensure that all persons receive ethical guidance, sex guidance, information concerning living together, and an offer of family planning. The object of these means is to 'develop a responsible attitude towards these matters such that the number of terminations of pregnancy will be as low as possible'. The Abortion Act played a central role in the development of health law as an early example of legislation giving the citizen entitlements, regardless of funding. The act also contains early examples of patient's rights (like information). The annual number of abortions has been decreasing in recent years. In 2021, 10,841 abortions were carried out in Norway (9.2 abortions per 1000 women aged 15–49).[129]

282. Should a pregnancy lead to serious difficulties for a woman, she is entitled to 'information and guidance' concerning the assistance which the society can offer her, cf. section 2, second paragraph. If a woman considers an abortion, she shall be given information regarding 'the nature of the intervention and its medical effects', cf. section 5, second paragraph. This provision is needless after the introduction of general rules concerning information in PRA Chapter 3, but was given before this later development (*see also* section 14a on follow-up in forms of guidance concerning contraceptive measures for women having underwent an abortion). If the woman, after being given guidance according to section 2, first paragraph and information according to section 5, second paragraph finds that she is nevertheless unable to complete the pregnancy to term, she shall 'herself make the final decision' concerning termination of pregnancy provided that it is possible to perform the operation before 'the twelfth week of pregnancy has elapsed', and that there are 'no serious reasons' to the contrary. The latter is seldom used as reason for denial. The term 'the twelfth week of pregnancy' gives room for a leeway. The ministry has issued a regulation (15 June 2001 No. 635), where the commentary implicitly takes last menstruation as a starting point, in addition to establishing thresholds based on ultrasound measurements. Surveys indicate that women may be managed differently depending on where they are referred for a pregnancy termination.[130]

---

128. For a legal analysis of abortion, *see* Aslak Syse, *Abortloven. Juss og verdure (Abortion Act: Law and Values)* (Gyldendal 1993).
129. *See* figures from Norwegian Institute of Public Health, https://www.fhi.no/hn/statistikk/statistikk3/abort---fakta-med-statistikk/ (accessed 10 Jul. 2022).
130. *See* M.J. Beiske, L. Næss og & P. Bergsjø, *Selvbestemt abort – ulik fortolkning av '12 fullgåtte uker' (Self-Decided Abortion – Different Interpretations of 12 Weeks of Gestation)* 126 Tidsskrift for den norske lægeforening (J. Norwegian Med. Assn.) 1738–1739 (2006).

283. After the twelfth week of pregnancy has elapsed, the pregnancy may be terminated if the conditions stipulated in section 2, third paragraph are fulfilled. The alternatives refer to the woman's medical condition (litra a), her social condition (litra b), eugenic conditions of the foetus (litra c), ethical circumstances (litra d), for example, the pregnancy is a result of rape or incest), or her mental condition, which must be of a severe degree (litra e). When assessing a request for termination of pregnancy according to litra a)–c), account shall 'be taken of the women's overall situation', cf. section 2, fourth paragraph. Major consideration 'shall be given' to the woman's 'own assessment of her situation'. The condition for termination of pregnancy shall 'become more stringent' as duration of pregnancy increases, cf. section 2, fifth paragraph. A pregnancy may not be terminated 'after the eighteenth week of pregnancy' unless there are 'particular important grounds' for doing so, cf. section 2, fifth paragraph, first sentence. If there is reason to believe that the foetus is 'viable', authorization for a pregnancy termination 'shall not be granted', cf. section 2, fifth paragraph, second sentence. The term 'viable' is elaborated in the regulation (15 June 2001 No. 635) section 18. According to this provision a foetus is viable if it will be able to survive outside the mother at the time of intervention. The possibility of treatment after birth shall be taken into consideration. It caused a public debate after physicians and midwives reported cases of foetus with heart activity being left to die. The Norwegian Directorate of Health issued a circular for the decision on these cases, and the regulation was amended (5 December 2014, No. 1510). According to the regulation section 18, last sentence, a foetus is to be considered liable after twenty-second week of pregnancy, unless special circumstances apply. Regardless of whether the foetus is viable, a pregnancy can be terminated according to section 10. In cases where the pregnancy constitutes 'an impending risk to the women's life or health', it may be terminated 'without regard to the provisions of this act'.

284. Abortion after the elapse of twelfth week pursuant to section 2, third paragraph is decided by a board consisting of two physicians, which shall make their decision after consultation with the woman, cf. section 7, second paragraph. The decision shall be in writing, cf. section 8. In the event that the application is rejected, the board shall inform the woman that the decision will be examined by the national board, unless she withdraws the application. The national board shall consist of five members, whereof at least two members shall be physicians and one a lawyer, cf. section 8, third paragraph. Several issues concerning abortion has been on the political agenda recently, partly when it came to the public that abortion was carried out for in cases of selective reduction, cf. section 2a (amendment 21 June 2019 No. 44). According to this provision, selective reduction should be considered as an abortion and may only be carried out after a board decision. The government has appointed an expert committee to review the Abortion Act, and especially the board system. .

285. An application for termination of pregnancy shall be submitted by the woman herself, cf. section 4. If she is under 16 years of age, the person exercising parental responsibility or guardian shall be given an opportunity to express his/her views, unless there 'are particular reasons to the contrary', cf. section 4, first paragraph, second sentence. The provision also regulates representation of women with mental incapacities. If the woman is under 16 years of age, and the person exercising parental responsibility has expressed the view that the pregnancy should not be terminated, the consent of the county governor, cf. section 9. This provision also regulates decision procedures of women with mental incapacities.

286. The regional health enterprises shall organize hospital services such that women in the area may have a pregnancy termination performed at any time, cf. section 14. The organization shall take into account that the health personnel who, 'for reason of conscience', do not wish to perform or assist in such situation.[131] According to the regulation (15 June 2001 No. 635) section health personnel with reason of conscience shall be exempted. This entitlement does not apply to personnel providing care before, during and after the intervention. A public debate took place in 2013/2014 after the ministry sent on hearing a draft introducing a possibility for general practitioners to make a reservation of referrals for termination of pregnancy, but the proposition was withdrawn.

§2. Sterilization

287. Sterilization is regulated by the Sterilisation Act (1977), which also covers castration. The act does not apply on intervention or treatment justified by medical or other grounds, cf. section 1. Like the Abortion Act, the Sterilisation Act has played a role in the development of health law, as being an area early subject of legalization with entitlements for the patients. The act was amended in 2006 (30 June 2006 No. 44), as part of the adjustments to the Council of Europe Convention on Protection of Human Rights and Dignity of the Human Being with regard to the Application of Biology and Medicine (Oviedo Convention).

288. Every person having reached the age of 25 years can be sterilized based upon application, cf. section 2. This does not apply to persons having a serious mental disorder or being mentally disabled or cognitive impaired. A person not fulfilling the requirements in section 2, can after application be given permission to be sterilized based on conditions stipulated in section 3:

(a) pregnancy or birth for a woman who applies can seriously jeopardize her life or physical or mental health;
(b) caring for a child could put the applicant in a difficult living condition;
(c) due to hereditary qualities by the applicant it is significant risk that an offspring will have a serious disease or blemish; or
(d) the applicant due to mental disorder or mentally disability or cognitive impairment will not be able to give sufficient care for a child.

---

131. For an analysis of the Swedish regulation in this matter, with comparison to Norway and Denmark, *see* Kavot Zillén, *Hälso- och sjukvårdspersonalens religions- och samvetsfrihet (Health Care Professionals' Freedom of Religion and Belief),* (Uppsala 2016).

Sterilization cannot be allowed on persons less than 18 years of age, except under extraordinary circumstances.

289. An application for sterilization is submitted by the person requiring the intervention. Is the person under 18 years of age or having a serious mental disorder or being mentally disabled or cognitive impaired, consent is also needed from the guardian, cf. section 4. The guardian can also submit an application on behalf of persons having a serious mental disorder or being mentally disabled or cognitive impaired, if the person concerned does not have the ability to decide on the matter and that it is unlikely that he or she in the future will be able to take such a decision.

290. An application for sterilization pursuant to section 2 is submitted to a physician, cf. section 5, first paragraph. An application for sterilization pursuant to section 3 is submitted to a physician or the sterilization board, cf. section 5, second paragraph. The decision is taken by the board. If a guardian has submitted an application on behalf of another pursuant to section 4, second paragraph, a permission for sterilization pursuant to section 3, litra c) or d) should only be granted if sterilization is clearly the best alternative to prevent a pregnancy for the person concerned, cf. section 5, second paragraph.

291. The person applying for sterilization shall be given information about the intervention, risk and medical impact, and other ways to prevent pregnancy, cf. section 5, third paragraph. The physician carrying out the intervention shall assure that such information is given. The provision is an example of early legalization of patient information, although it could now be considered as redundant besides the general rules in PRA Chapter 3.

292. The sterilization board shall consist of the county governor – or whom he appoints – and two other members appointed by the King, cf. section 6, second paragraph. The sterilization council consists of a physician as chairman and four other members, whereas one judge and two physicians, cf. section 6, first paragraph. The sterilization council is appeal body where the sterilization board has rejected applications pursuant to section 3.

293. There are annually between twenty and thirty decisions according to section 3 (statistics are not published). There has been a significant decrease in sterilization pursuant to section 2. This development is probably due to changes in the fees to be paid by the patients, combined with other means for prevention and long waiting lists for sterilization within the public system. The fee to be paid by the patients if the intervention is carried out within the public health system is NOK 6,079 (approx. EUR 600) for women and NOK 1,268 (approx. EUR 120) for men. There are exemptions for this fee, i.e., if it is carried out on women already being in hospital giving birth. The different treatment of the genders has been subject to political debate and to legal controversies. When incorporating the UN Convention on the Elimination of All Forms of Discrimination against Women in the Human Rights Act, the ministry made the assessment that unequal treatment was in conformity with the convention.[132]

294. Persons with an abnormal sex drive who likely would commit sexual offences can be castrated after application, cf. section 8. This kind of intervention has not been carried out in recent years, but some offenders have been offered medication impacting their sex drive (which requires their consent pursuant to the PRA section 4-1).

§3. In Vitro Fertilization

295. In vitro fertilization is regulated by the Biotechnology Act (2003) section 2. This part of the act contains regulation of medically assisted reproduction (defined as 'insemination and in vitro fertilization'), insemination (defined as 'the introduction of sperm into a woman's body by means other than sexual intercourse) and in vitro fertilization (defined as 'fertilization of oocytes (eggs) outside a woman's body'), cf. section 2-1. The use of medically assisted reproduction was previously permitted only if the woman is 'married' or 'living in a stable relationship resembling marriage', cf. section 2-2. The latter contained previously the amendment 'with a man', but this was deleted when introducing same sex marriage (amendment 27 June 2008 No. 53). After a political debate, medically assisted reproduction is also provided to single women now (amendment 19 June 2020 No. 78). Only women who live alone are considered to be single, cf. section 2-2. The amendments in 2020 also led to other forms of liberalization of the legislation.

296. Insemination may only take place if the man is infertile or suffers from or is a carrier of a serious hereditary disease, when the woman are married or are living in a stable relationship resembling marriage, or to a single women, cf. section 2-3. Additionally, insemination can take place when a man or woman is contagious of a serious and chronically sexual transmittable infection. In special cases, insemination may take place if the woman is a carrier of a serious sex-linked hereditary disease, cf. also section 2-13. In vitro fertilization may only take place if the woman or man is 'infertile' or 'in the case of infertility for which no cause has been identified', cf. section 2-4.

297. When the legislation was amended in 2020, an age limit for women was also introduced. According to section 2-3a, the women who receives medically assisted reproduction cannot be older than 46 years.

298. The women, or in case also her partner, shall be given 'information on the treatment and on the medical and legal consequences it may have', cf. section 2-5,

132. Ot.prp. No. 93 (2008–2009) *Om lov om endringar i menneskerettsloven mv. (inkorporering av kvinnediskrimineringskonvensjonen) (Regarding Act Amending the Human Rights Act (Incorporating the Convention on the Elimination of Discrimination against Women)),* 31–32.

first paragraph. This 'shall include information on adoption'. Before the treatment is started, the physician who is providing the treatment shall ensure that 'written' consent is obtained from the woman, or in case also her partner, cf. section 2-5, second paragraph. This is one of the few provisions in Norwegian Health Law requiring a written consent. If the treatment is repeated, 'renewed consent shall be obtained'. Only persons over the age of 18 years who are not being declared legally incapable in personal matters can give such consent. The provision addresses the situation where donor sperm is used and the women has had a new partner during the process, and the new partner must also consent, cf. section 2-5, third paragraph. A consent from the former partner is not required.

299. The decision to undertake treatment with a view to medically assisted reproduction shall be 'taken by a physician', cf. section 2-6. The decision shall be based on medical and psychosocial assessment of the couple. Importance shall be attached to the couple's capacity to provide parental care and the best interests of the child. The physician 'may obtain any information necessary' to make an overall assessment of the couple. Confidential information may only be collected with the consent of the couple. Everyone seeking for medically assisted reproduction are required to submit a police certificate of conduct, cf. section 2-6, second paragraph.

300. Parents to a child born by donation of unfertilized oocytes or donated sperm shall as soon as advisable inform the child. Any person who is born as a result of such medically assisted reproduction 'has a right to information on the sperm donor's identity at the age of 15', cf. section 2-7. This provision has been object of controversy. Previously, sperm donors were anonymous. Norway received comments from the committee supervising the UN Convention on the Rights of the Child observing the 'possible contradiction between the Convention and in keeping the identity of sperm donors secret'.[133] The relevant provision is Article 7, which gives the child 'the right to know and be cared for by his or her parents'. This criticism lead to an amendment of the previous Biotechnology Act, although it may be uncertain how Article 7 should be interpreted and how far-reaching to obligation is under the convention. The identity requirement has led to a decrease in men volunteering for donation and an increase in couples going abroad to have insemination in countries offering anonymity (like Denmark). Until the amendment in 2020, the age limit was 18 years, and this still applies to children born before the amendment.

301. A sperm donor 'shall have reached the legal age of majority', cf. section 2-9, first paragraph. An oocyte donor must be over the age of 25 and not older than 35 years, cf. section 2-9, second paragraph. In both cases the donor must not be deprived of his/her capacity in personal matters. The donor must give 'written consent' for the oocyte/sperm to be used for fertilization and for his identity to be recorded in the donor register (as stipulated in section 2-8). Consent may be withdrawn 'until fertilization has taken place'. A sperm 'shall not be given information'

133. CRC/C/15/Add.23, para. 10 (1994).

on the couple's or the child's identity, cf. section 2-9, second paragraph. The physician who is providing the treatment shall select 'a suitable oocyte donor or sperm donor', cf. section 2-10.

302. Treatment of sperm before fertilization for the purpose of selecting the sex of the child is only permitted if 'the woman is a carrier of a serious sex-linked hereditary disease', cf. section 2-13. Embryos may only be used for implantation into the woman from 'whom the oocytes were obtained', cf. section 2-15, first paragraph. In cases of medically assisted reproduction of single women, the oocytes must be harvested from to women herself, cf. section 2-15, second paragraph. In cases of medically assisted reproduction to couples, simultaneous oocyte and sperm donation is not allowed, cf. section 2-15, third paragraph, nor donation of fertilized eggs. In cases of assisted reproduction to female couples, an oocyte that is harvested from one of the partners can be inseminated into the other partner after fertilization, cf. section 2-15, fourth paragraph.

303. Previously, it was a time limit of five years for the storage of fertilized oocytes. The storage time is now unlimited, cf. section 2-16. Still, it can be shortened due to capacity but not less than five years unless the woman consents. However, the woman must be under the age of 46 years at the time of insemination.

304. Previously, the use of sperm after the donor had diseased was prohibited. Section 2-17 now states that sperm from a diseased or oocytes fertilized with the diseased sperm, may be used for medically assisted reproduction if it is documented that this was in line with the wishes of the diseased. The surviving partner must be single and the other conditions for medically assisted reproduction must be fulfilled. In case of the use of fertilized oocytes, the oocyte must come from the surviving partner.

305. The transplantation of gamete-producing organs and tissue from one person to another for the purpose of treating infertility is prohibited, cf. section 2-18, first paragraph.

306. The use of unfertilized oocytes and embryos for education and quality assurance is regulated by section 2-14 (for research on embryos, *see* Chapter 3). Such use can only be made if the couple or single woman has given a voluntary, explicit and informed consent, cf. section 2-14, third paragraph.

307. While most forms of treatment are under the autonomy of the health personnel and institutions, all forms of treatment, storage and import are to be approved by the Norwegian Directorate of Health, cf. section 2-19 (delegated from the ministry). Before approval, the application shall be reviewed by the Norwegian Biotechnology Advisory Board, cf. section 2-19, second paragraph.

§4. PRENATAL DIAGNOSIS (GENETICS IN GENERAL)

308. Prenatal diagnosis, as well genetics in general, is regulated by the above-mentioned Biotechnology Act (2003). This was replacing the former Biotechnology Act (1994), which in turn replaced the Artificial Insemination Act, being the first legislation in the field. The rapid scientific development has led to continuous amendments in the legislation, and has significantly reduced the average living age of the legislation.

309. The purpose of the Biotechnology Act is according to section 1-1 to ensure that medical applications of biotechnology are utilized for 'the benefit of everyone in an inclusive society'. This shall be done in accordance with the principles of respect for 'human dignity, human rights and personal integrity and without any discrimination' on the basis of genetic constitution, on the basis of the ethical norms that form part of 'our Western cultural heritage'. Many of the phrases in the purpose section is praising words commonly used in contemporary legislation, but the reference to 'Western cultural heritage' is a particularity (inherited from the 1994 Act).

310. The act applies to the application of biotechnology in human medicine, etc., including medically assisted reproduction, research on embryos and cloning, prenatal diagnosis, postnatal genetic testing, gene therapy, etc., cf. section 1-2, first paragraph. The act does not apply to research unless the participants are to receive healthcare or individual feedback of results of genetic examinations, cf. section 2-1, second paragraph (with exception from the provisions of Chapter 3). The Act does not apply to autopsies that come within the scope of the Transplant Act (*see* §6 *infra*) and the provisions on expert autopsies according to the Criminal Procedure Code, cf. section 1-2, third paragraph.

311. Chapter 2A was introduced in 2007 in order to open up for a limited use of genetic testing of embryos prior to inserting in uterus (pre-implementation diagnostic), cf. amendment 15 June 2007 No. 31. Major revisions were made in 2020. Previously, all treatment had to be approved by a committee but this system was abolished by an amendment. Pre-implementation diagnostic may only be provided to couples where one or both are carrier of a specific hereditary disease and where it is very likely that the disease will be transferred to the offspring, cf. section 2A-1, first paragraph. Additionally, pre-implementation diagnostic may be carried in order to examine type of tissue with the aim of having a child which can be stem cell donor for a sibling with serious, heredity disease, cf. section 2A-1, third paragraph. This provision was indeed controversial, with a large minority in the parliament. Pre-implementation diagnostic cannot be used in order to chart or select other characteristic by the embryo, than those stipulated in section 2A-1, cf. fourth paragraph. Genetic modification of the embryo is prohibited, cf. section 2A-1, fifth paragraph.

312. Prior to the pre-implementation diagnostic, the couple must give a written, informed consent, cf. section 2A-2. Before submitting application, the couple shall receive neutral information and genetic counselling, including information regarding risk related to the treatment, the strain for the woman and the probability of success, cf. section 2A-3. This provision is to a large extent redundant besides the regulation in PRA section 3, although more specific.

313. Chapter 3 contains provisions regarding research on supernumerary embryos, and the amendment in 2007 abolished the prohibition against research on embryos. Only research satisfying the purposes stipulated in section 3-1 can be carried out. Additionally, research must be carried out no later than fourteen days after fertilization, and oocytes cannot be fertilized only for research purposes, cf. section 3-2. Research on embryos and cells deriving from embryos may only take place after prior approval of a regional committee of medical and health research ethics, cf. section 3-3, first paragraph. New forms of treatment requiring use of cells from embryos shall be approved by the Ministry, cf. section 3-3, second paragraph. Prior to such a decision, the application shall be reviewed by the Norwegian Biotechnology Advisory Board, cf. section 3-3, third paragraph. This political review of offered treatment is rather rare, but must be seen in the light of the particular ethical challenges in the field. Research on embryos may only take place after a voluntary, explicit and informed consent by the couple, cf. section 3-4 (and if appropriate also the donor). Creating human embryos by cloning is prohibited, cf. section 3-5. The prohibition also included research on techniques, cf. section 3-6.

314. Prenatal diagnosis is regulated by Chapter 4. A definition of prenatal diagnosis is given in section 4-1, which explicitly omits ultrasound examination, cf. section 4-1, second paragraph. However, one provision applies also on ultrasound examination. Information on the sex of the foetus before the twelfth week of pregnancy may only be given if the woman is a carrier of a serious sex-linked disease, cf. section 4-5. The time limit is given in order to correspond with the deadline for self-determined abortion, cf. *supra* §1.

315. Methods of examination that come within the scope of Chapter 4 shall be authorized by the Ministry. In line with the procedures under Chapter 3, the application shall be submitted by the Norwegian Biotechnology Advisory Board, cf. section 4-2. Before prenatal diagnosis, written consent shall be obtained from the person who is to be examined, cf. section 4-3. The consent shall be based on information and genetic counselling, cf. section 4-4.

316. Prenatal paternity testing is prohibited, cf. section 4-6. However, this provision does not apply when the pregnancy may be a result of certain sexual offences (with referral to specific provision in the Penal Code).

317. By amendment of 7 May 2015 No. 25 a new Chapter 4A was inserted in the Biotechnology Act regarding the use of foetus tissue (in force from 1 January 2016). A regulation of this matter was previously found in the act relating to transplantation, hospital autopsies and the donation of bodies (1973), and the transferal to the Biotechnology Act chapter came as a result of the new Transplantation Act, cf. section 6 *infra*. Chapter 4A is regulating use of cells and tissue from provoked abortions, cf. section 4A-1. The term 'foetus tissue' will be used in the following text. Foetus tissue can only be used for 'medical research, diagnostic, make out of vaccine and treatment', cf. section 4A-2, second paragraph. Such use is only allowed in case of serious disease or injury, and where other forms of treatment have limited effect, cf. section 4A-2, second paragraph. The use of foetus tissue for 'medical research, diagnostic, make out of vaccine' is only allowed if other equal methods are not available, cf. section 4A-2, second paragraph, last sentence. It is prohibited to use ovary tissue from aborted foetuses' for transplant, cf. section 4A-2, third paragraph. Commercial utilization of foetus tissue is prohibited, cf. section 4A-2, fourth paragraph. Use of foetus tissue for treatment and research shall be approved by the ministry, cf. section 4A-3. A written consent must be obtained from the woman, based on sufficient information, cf. section 4A-4. All collection, storage and hand out of foster tissue should be made by a foetus tissue bank, approved by the ministry, cf. section 4A-5. The female donor and receiver of foetus tissue shall not know each other's identity, cf. section 4A-6. Everyone receiving foetus tissue shall be informed that the material stems from tissue obtained after a provoked abortion, cf. section 4A-7. Similar to the regulation concerning abortion, cf. *supra* section 1, health personnel can for reason of conscience object to participate in research projects where foetus tissue is used, or in conducting or assisting by transplants of foetus tissue, cf. section 4A-8.

318. Chapter 5 regulates postnatal genetic testing, and was also revised in 2020. Genetic testing is defined as: (a) to diagnose a disease; (b) pre-symptomatic genetic testing, predictive genetic testing and testing to determine whether or not a person is a carrier of hereditary disease that will only be expressed in later generations (carrier testing); and (c) laboratory genetic testing to determine sex, with the exception of laboratory genetic testing for identification purposes, cf. section 5-1, second paragraph. This definition plays a vital role in Chapter 5, since many provisions only apply to testing pursuant to litra b).

319. Genetic testing shall only be carried out for 'medical purposes if it has a diagnostic or therapeutic objective', cf. section 5-2. Previously, it was stated that before genetic testing of the types listed in section 5-1, second paragraph, litra b) is carried out, the Ministry should give separate authorization for each disease or predisposition to a disease that is to be tested, cf. section 5-3, first. This procedure was abolished in 2020.

320. Before genetic testing that comes within the scope of section 5-1, second paragraph litra b) is carried out, written consent shall be examined, cf. section 5-4, which must be based on genetic counselling given 'before, during and after' genetic testing, cf. section 5-5. If the patient is under 16 years old, consent shall be contained from the parents or other representatives. Such genetic testing shall not be carried out on children under the age of 16 unless the test can detect a condition for which treatment may 'prevent or reduce damage to a child's health', cf. section 5-7. The provision gives the ministry the competence to 'in special cases' grant exemptions from this prohibition.

321. According to section 5-8 it is prohibited to 'request, receive, be in possession of or use information' on another person obtained through genetic testing that comes within the scope of section 5-1, second paragraph, litra b, or by systematic surveys of hereditary disease within a family. Additionally, it is prohibited to ask whether genetic testing or systematic surveys of hereditary disease within a family have been carried out. The prohibition does not apply to establishments that are authorized pursuant to section 7-1 to carry out genetic, or for research purposes, cf. section 5-8, third paragraph. The provision explicitly states that if genetic information is to be used for research purposes, consent must have been obtained from the person from whom the information was obtained. Finally, health personnel who need the information for 'diagnostic and therapeutic purposes' are exempted from the prohibition of the first and second paragraphs, cf. section 5-8, fourth paragraph.

322. Section 5-9 contains provisions regarding the information flow of the outcome of genetic testing. If it has been documented that a patient suffers from or has a predisposition to a hereditary disease, the starting point is that the 'patient himself' may decide whether or not to inform at-risk relatives of his condition, cf. section 5-9, second paragraph. However, for specific disease selected by the ministry, information can be passed on to relatives even if the patient does not consent in 'special cases', cf. section 5-9, fourth paragraph. Additionally, health personnel can pass on information if the patient prefers not to carry out this task, or is unable to do so. Before health personnel contacts the relatives, they shall according to section 5-9, sixth paragraph assess whether:

(1) the disease in question 'has serious consequences' for the individual's life or health;
(2) there is a 'reasonable probability' that the person's relatives are also genetically predisposed to the disease and may develop the disease later in life;
(3) there is 'a documented link' between genetic predisposition to the disease and the development of the disease;
(4) the genetic tests used to determine whether a person carries a genetic predisposition to the disease are 'reliable'; and
(5) there are 'satisfactory methods' of 'preventing or treating' the disease.

323. Regarding direct to consumer genetic testing, the ministry stated in the preparatory work that if genetic self-testing would introduced, the ministry would ascertain that they only would be provided by enterprises with approval according to the act.[134] Furthermore, the ministry announced that they would closely follow the development of direct to consumer genetic testing and take appropriate measures to limit the availability. In 2014, a Swedish company offered self-testing from pharmacies in Norway, besides from their website. The Norwegian Directorate of Health held that pharmacies offering self-testing should not been considered as

134. Ot.prp. No. 64 (2002–2003) *Om lov om medisinsk bruk av bioteknologi m.m. (bioteknologiloven) (Regarding Act Relating to the Application of Biotechnology in Human Medicine, Etc. (Biotechnology Act)),* 89.

'medical use' of biotechnology, and hence falling outside the scope of the Biotechnology Act.[135] As a consequence, these pharmacies were not obliged to require an authorization according to section 7-1. In their reply, the ministry stated their consensus regarding the scope of the act. However, they stressed that the prohibition in section 5-8 still applied. It may seem as a bit contradictory at the same state both that the Biotechnology Act does not apply and that certain prohibition is targeting the same activity that falls outside the scope. The ministry emphasized that the prohibition in section 5-8 also applies when the analysis are made abroad, as long as the samples are taken in Norway. The Control of Marketing and Contract Terms Act apply also on direct to consumer genetic testing. After a commercial in a daily newspaper from a Danish provider offering genetic tests for children (a picture of a child with angel wings followed by the text that all angels should be genetically tested) a case was instituted by the Consumer Ombudsperson.[136] In the Ombudsman's opinion the advertising was in an unfair manner allude to the parent's fair for the children's possible diseases, Furthermore, the Ombudsman also expressed the opinion that the advertising was misleading since it was stating that the tests would provide reliable answers. The company was therefore requested to withdraw the marketing campaign. When the legislation was amended in 2020, the ministry discussed in the preparatory works whether a prohibition of genetic self-testing should be introduced.[137] The ministry proposed not do so, and emphasized that such a regulation could be in conflict with EEA obligations and that the test itself did not pose a health risk. Under the process in the parliament, the standing committee for health and care affairs asked the government to return with a proposal to prohibit genetic self-testing.[138]

324. Gene therapy is regulated by Chapter 6. The definition in section 6-1 refers to Regulation 1394/2007 (EC) on advanced therapy medicinal products, cf. Directive 2001/83/EC on Community Node relating to medicinal products for human use. Gene therapy may only be used 'to treat serious diseases or to prevent the occurrence of such diseases', cf. section 6-2, first paragraph. Gene therapy on 'foetuses and embryos' and gene therapy 'that may involve genetic modification of gametes' is prohibited, cf. section 6-2, second paragraph. Previously, methods of treatment that come within the scope of section 6-2, first paragraph, should be authorized by the ministry, cf. section 6-3, first paragraph. This procedure was abolished when the legislation was amended in 2020. Before gene therapy is carried out, 'written consent' shall be obtained from the person who is to be treated, cf. section 6-4. The provision does not contain specific regulation regarding consent, and the general rules in PRA section 3 will therefore apply. Before gene therapy involving a child under the age of 16 is started, written consent shall be obtained from the child's parents or another person who has parental responsibility, cf. section 6-4, last sentence.

---

135. Letter to the Ministry of Health and Care, dated 21 Aug. 2014, ref. 14/7114-2.
136. *See* opinion 11 May 2012, ref. 12/634-2.
137. Prop.34 L (2019–2020) *Endringer i bioteknologiloven mv (Amendments of the Biotechnology Act)* 47–50.
138. Innst.296 L (2019–2020) *Innstilling fra helse- og omsorgskomiteen om Endringer i bioteknologiloven mv (Recommendation by the health and care committee regarding amendments of the Biotechnology Act)* 15–16.

325. Any person that wilfully contravenes the Biotechnology Act or provisions laid down pursuant thereto is liable to fines or to a term of imprisonment not exceeding three months, cf. section 7-5. An accomplice is 'liable to the same penalties', cf. the Penal Code section 15. However, the penal provisions does not apply to: (a) 'private persons' seeking or using methods violation the act; (b) those donating oocytes, sperm or fertilized eggs; or (c) research participants, cf. section 7-5, second paragraph. This provision was taken into the act after an amendment (21 June 2013 No. 78). In the preparatory work this amendment was presented as a clarification, although it could be argued that the additional provision in reality was a substantial alteration.[139] However, currently the legal situation is clear for private persons (e.g., going abroad for surrogacy).

326. The Biotechnology Act is an example of an area in health law with frequent changes, often related to public debates and political controversies. Partly as a response to this, the Norwegian Biotechnology Advisory Board is instituted as a body to facilitate the discussions and to provide guidance for the authorities, cf. section 7-3.[140] The board consists of fifteen members. The board shall on request or on its own initiative give opinions on matters that come within the scope of this Act and other questions relating to biotechnology. The opinions of the board are public unless otherwise required by the statutory duty of confidentiality.

§5. Psycho Surgical Interventions

327. Psycho surgical intervention in form of lobotomy was carried out in Norway. An expert committee scrutinizing the practice estimates that about 2,500 lobotomies were made in Norway between 1941 and 1974 (and most of them until the 1950s).[141] This surgical intervention was much more frequent in Norway compared with Sweden and higher than in the UK and USA, but in line with Denmark. The legal basis for the intervention was the principle of necessity, based on an analogy of the Penal Code. In the preparatory work to an amendment to the former MHA in 1981, it has been taken as *de lege lata* that lobotomy could only be carried out based on an informed consent from the patient. All remaining victims of the practice of lobotomy granted compensation by the state (same amount to all former patients). The scheme was enabled by decision in parliament.

328. There are no specific provisions in the legislation prohibiting lobotomy or other forms of psycho surgical interventions. The legal starting point will be the consent from the patient, based on sufficient information. Additionally, the intervention must be in conformity with the requirement of responsible conduct, cf. HPA

139. Prop.95 L (2012–2013) *Endringer i bioteknologiloven (straffebestemmelsen og assistert befruktning til personer med seksuelt overførbare sykdommer) (Amendments to the Biotechnology Act (The Criminal Provision and Assisted Fertilization to Persons Suffering from Sexual Transmitted Diseases)),* 20–21.
140. The board has a website with some information in English, *see* http://www.bioteknologiradet.no/english/ (accessed 10 Jul. 2022).
141. NOU 1992:25 *Utredning om lobotomi (Report Regarding Lobotomy).*

section 4. Lobotomy would not meet the latter requirement, but other psycho surgical the profession as responsible conduct may in the future consider intervention. In this assessment, the irreversibility of the intervention will be a crucial point.

§6. ORGAN TRANSPLANTS

329. From 1 January 2016, the Transplantation Act (2015) and the Autopsy Act (2015) replaces the former act relating to transplantation, hospital autopsies and donation of bodies (1973). An expert committee drafted a proposal for a new act,[142] which the ministry to a large extent based their proposition on.[143] The parliament passed the act without alteration, and only a few issues were object of controversies.

330. The Transplantation Act regulates both donation and transplantation of organs, as well as cells and tissue. Regarding cells and tissue the act is implementing Directive 2004/23/EC on setting standards of quality and safety for the donation, procurement, testing, processing, preservation, storage and distribution of human tissues and cells. The objects of the Transplantation Act is to secure the best possible access of organs, cells and tissue for treatment of humans, respect the will and integrity of the donor and protect the interests of the next in kin, cf. section 1. The ambit of the act is donation, transplant and similar use of living, human organ, cells and tissue from a living or dead donor with the purpose of treatment of disease or injury of another person, cf. section 2. The act does not apply to blood and tissue use in relation to reproduction and human organs, cells and tissue only used in research. The responsibility for facilitating for donation is vested with the regional health enterprises, cf. section 4. The act is divided in three main chapters, besides the introductory chapter. Donation from a living is regulated by Chapter 3, donation from dead donor is regulated by Chapter 3 and common requirements are found in Chapter 4.

331. Removal from a living donor of organs, cells and tissue can only be carried out if the intervention does not represent a nearby risk for the physical or mental health of the donor, cf. section 5, first paragraph. Requirements of removal from persons between 12 and 18 years are stipulated in section 5, second paragraph. Such intervention can only be carried out if 'special reasons' apply, and the provision contains guidance for factors to be taken into consideration. Requirements of removal from donors under the age of 12 years and for adults without the competence to give consent is found in section 5, third paragraph. These are stricter than for persons between 12 and 18 years. Only renewable tissue can be removed and the donation must be necessary in order to save the life of the receiver. Additionally, a donor with

142. NOU 2011:21 *Når døden tjener livet. Et forslag til nye lover om transplantasjon, obduksjon og avgivelse av lik (When Death Serves Life: A Draft for New Acts Relating to Transplantation, Autopsy and the Donation of Bodies).*
143. Prop.38 L (2014–2015) *Transplantasjonslov og obduksjonslov (Transplantation Act and Autopsy Act).*

the competence to consent must not be available and receiver must be in close family with the donor. A removal can never be carried out if a donor without the competence to consent objects thereto, cf. section 5, fourth paragraph.

332. A written consent is required for removal of organs, cells and tissue from a living donor, cf. section 6, first paragraph. The consent shall also include the processing of health information that is necessary to carry out to implement the intervention. The consent can be withdrawn, cf. section 6, second paragraph. Provisions regarding the competence to consent are given in section 7. Persons over the age of 18 have the right to consent to donation, cf. section 7, first paragraph. For persons under the age of 18, the parents, or others holding the parental responsibility pursuant the Children Act, have the competence to consent. The age limit is here higher than the general rule established by PRA section 4-3. A donation cannot take place if the parents disagree, cf. section 7, second paragraph. For persons lacking the competence to consent pursuant to PRA section 4-3, second paragraph, the closest next of kin is entitled to consent on behalf of the donor. While the next of kin in other health issues is to a limited extent given the competence to give a represented consent, the next of kin plays a more central role regarding donations. For person lacking the competence to act in personal matters pursuant to the Guardian Act section 22, the guardian shall consent, cf. section 7, fourth paragraph with referral to PRA section 4-7. A represented consent must be approved by the county governor, cf. section 7, fourth paragraph. The aim is to provide for an independent assessment in order to protect the donor's interests.

333. In order for a consent to be valid, the donor and the person representing the donor must have been provided with information according to section 7. This provision is more detailed than the general regulation in PRA section 3. Partly, more comprehensive information is required due to the consequences of the intervention. However, section 7 is also partly a modernization of the general provisions, i.e., when emphasizing the cultural and linguistic background. Donors are entitled to necessary medical and psychological examination prior to giving consent, and also post follow-up, cf. section 9.

334. Section 8 addresses the health personnel. The person responsible for the patient in need of a transplant shall not solely conduct the assessment of whether the donor is suitable. This rule is required in order to have an independent review taking into account the possible conflicting interests.

335. The provisions in Chapter 3 concerning donation from a dead donor starts with a regulation of death. A removal cannot be carried out before the death is confirmed by a physician, cf. section 10, first paragraph. In order to secure an independent assessment, the physician making this assessment shall not be involved in the removal of organs, cells and tissue or the transplant surgery, cf. section 10, second paragraph. If the death is confirmed by an irreversible cease of brain functions, the diagnosis must be confirmed by two physicians, whereas at least one should be a specialist, cf. section 10, third paragraph. When death is confirmed, or it is very likely that the person will die in the near future and life supporting treatment is without purpose, an assessment of whether the patient can be a donor 'shall' be carried out, cf. section 11. This obligation for the hospital was an innovation compared with previous legislation.

336. When life supporting treatment is without purpose, and it is very likely that the patient will die in the near future, the physician responsible for the patient can make a decision of providing treatment in order to facilitate a donation, cf. section 12, first paragraph. Such treatment cannot be given if one of the closest next of kin refuses. The physician shall in cooperation with the next of kin make an assessment of the duration of the treatment facilitating a donation, cf. section 12, second paragraph. It shall nevertheless end when it is clarified that the condition for a donation is not fulfilled.

337. Persons over the age of 16 years are entitled to consent to donation of organs, cells and tissue, which are to be carried out after their death, cf. section 13, first paragraph. When the deceased has given consent, the next of kin cannot object to a donation. If the deceased has not given consent, a donation can be carried out if there are no circumstances that indicate that the deceased would have objected thereto, cf. section 13, second paragraph. The next of kin should be asked of such circumstances. Donation shall not be carried out if one of the closest next of kin objects thereto or if it is impossible to obtain contact with the next of kin, or of the deceased to not have next of kin. For persons under the age of 16, the parents, or others holding the parental responsibility pursuant the Children Act, have the competence to consent. The age limit for donation from deceased is here in line with the general rule established by PRA section 4-3. A donation cannot take place if the parents disagree, cf. section 13, third paragraph.

338. The closest next of kin shall be informed about the death, the planned removal and the entitlements to object to donation, cf. section 14, first paragraph. As far as possible, the next of kin shall have time to take one's leave with their relative prior to the removal, cf. section 15.

339. Assignments of organs, tissue cells and for transplantation shall be based on medical considerations, cf. section 16, first sentence. However, in cases of donation from a living donor the family connection can be taken into account, cf. section 16, second sentence. This provision is built on a principle of equal treatment, but is vesting the physicians with a wide discretion.

340. If the donor and receiver are not familiar with each other prior to the intervention, their identity shall not be revealed, cf. section 17. This condition of anonymity is similar as the provisions in the Biotechnology Act section 4A-6.

341. All expenses and compensation for loss of income occurring for a living donor or the closest next of kin of a dead donor shall be compensated by the regional health enterprise, cf. section 18. This reimbursement does not apply if the costs are covered pursuant to other provisions in the legislation. The coverage of expenses is a kind of acknowledgement from the society of the value of contributing. At the same time, there shall be no revenue to avoid the impression of sale of organs. Similar values are expressed in section 20. Every performance aiming for an economic gain of donation of organs, cells and tissue for transplant is prohibited.

342. Xenotransplantation – the transfer of living biological material from animals to humans is explicitly prohibited, cf. section 19.[144]

343. An enduring power of attorney pursuant to the Guardian Act Chapter 10 can cover both the consent and the refusal to donate organs, cells and tissue, cf. section 21. For decisions pursuant to section 9 (examination and follow-up) and section 18 (compensation for expenses), the complaint provisions in the PRA Chapter 7 applies, cf. section 22.

344. In 2013, 271 individuals were registered as potential donors in Norway. Of this, 111 were used. A total of 526 organs were transplanted to 467 patients. By the end of 2013, it was 365 patients on waiting list for donations, of them 266 for kidney transplant. The next of kin refrained from donation in 28% of the cases where they were asked about the opinion of the deceased, or their own opinion.[145]

345. The previous legislation (1973) differentiated between autopsy after death inside and outside of hospitals and other institutions. The current act (2015) is not built on a similar distinction, and applies to all forms of medical autopsy. Autopsy for investigation purposes in regulated by the Criminal Procedure Code. A medical autopsy can be carried out if it is not reason to believe that the deceased would have objected to the intervention, cf. section 7. A medical autopsy shall not be carried out if one of the closest next of kin objects thereto. Persons over the age of 18 years can in writing consent to the donation of the body for education and research after their death, cf. section 9, first paragraph. If the deceased had not consented, but it can be demonstrated that such a donation is in line with the wishes of the deceased, the next of kin can give a represented consent, cf. section 9, second paragraph.

§7. Experiments on Human Beings

346. One of the most renowned judgments in Norwegian Health Law was the criminal conviction of the physician Gerhard Henrik Armauer Hansen (1841–1912).[146] He became a well-known researcher for his discoveries concerning the leprosy disease (Mycobacterium leprae), being the first bacterium to be identified as causing disease in humans. In 1879, he planted material containing one form

144. *See also* NOU 2001:18 *Xenotransplantasjon. Medisinsk bruk av levende celler, vev og organer fra dyr (Xenotransplantation: Medical Use of Living Cells, Tissue and Organs from Animals).*

145. Prop.38 L (2014–2015) *Transplantasjonslov og obduksjonslov (Transplant Act and Autopsy Act)*, 10.

146. *See* Knut Blom, *Armauer Hansen and Human Leprosy Transmission Medical Ethics and Legal Rights*, 41 Intl. J. Leprosy & other Mycobacterial Diseases 199–207 (1973).

of leprosy into the eye of a woman suffering from another form of leprosy. Her consent was not obtained prior to the intervention. During the hearing Hansen explained that it could not be presumed that she had consented if he beforehand had given her information about the purpose of the intervention. He was convicted by the city court for causing her bodily harm (judgment 31 May 1880). As to the sentence, he was removed from the position as physician at the Leprosy hospital. However, there was no reason to extend the forfeiture to the position as Chief Medical Officer for leprosy, since his misconduct was not associated with the latter.

347. The first legislative approach was the regulation concerning medical trials (21 August 1981 No. 8835), which required an ethical assessment of the project and referred to the Helsinki declaration (section 10). A system of medical ethics committees was established in 1985, but this was done by administrative decisions and not stipulated by law. An expert committee reviewed medical trials in the period 1945–1975. The committee was appointed based on allegations of unethical conduct, but the committee did find proof of such incidents.[147] There were several calls for a regulation of the committee system based on legislation, and the debate regarding ethical issues in research was also fertilized by public debated case concerning scientific fraud. This lead to the introduction of the Ethics and Integrity in Research Act. This act is covering all fields of science and stipulated the establishment of national ethics committees. Within the field of medical and health research, the act also made regional ethics committee legally mandatory, replacing the former customary approach. The legislation concerning medical research was reviewed by an expert committee with the mandate of drafting an act for the field (2003–2004).[148] One of the findings was that the regulation was fragmented and being an impediment for medical research. The ministry drafted a proposition based on the committee's suggestions (with some alterations),[149] and the Health Research Act passed the parliament in 2008 (in force from 1 July 2009).[150]

348. One of the main purposes of the act was to establish a system of 'one mailbox' where the researcher should only relate to one body when applying for approval of medical research. The preparatory work paid significant attention to international instruments, both legal (like the Convention for the Protection of Human Rights and Dignity of the Human Being with regard to the Application of

---

147. NOU 2003:33 *Granskning av påstander om uetisk medisinsk forskning på mennesker – En granskning av påstander om uetisk medisinsk forskning med LSD, elektroder og radioaktiv stråling på mennesker i Norge i perioden 1945–1975 (Review of Allegations Regarding Unethical Research on Humans – A Review of Allegations Regarding Unethical Medical Research of LSD, Electrode and Radio Activation on Humans in Norway in 1945–1975).*
148. NOU 2005:1 *God forskning – bedre helse. Lov om medisinsk og helsefaglig forskning, som involverer mennesker, humant biologisk materiale og helseopplysninger (helseforskningsloven) (Good Research – Better Health: Act Relating to Medical and Health Research Involving Humans, Human Biological Material and Health Information (The Health Research Act)).*
149. Ot.prp. No. 74 (2006–2007) Om lov om medisinsk og helsefaglig forskning (helseforskningsloven) *(Regarding Act Relating to Medical and Health (The Health Research Act)).*
150. *See* Sigmund Simonsen & Magne Nylenna, *Ethical and Legal Regulation of Medical Research: Basic Principles and New Proposals for Norway*, 2 Scandinavian J. Work, Envt. & Health 5–14 (2006).

Biology and Medicine (Oviedo Convention) 4 April 1997) and professional norms (like the Helsinki declaration and Vancouver Convention). The purpose of the Health Research Act is to 'promote good and ethically sound medical and health research', cf. section 1.

349. The act applies to 'all medical and health research on human beings, human biological material or personal health data', cf. section 2, first paragraph. Such research also includes 'pilot studies and experimental treatments'. The act does not apply to establishment of health registers, cf. section 2, second paragraph. Such issues are regulated by the Health Register Act. Unless otherwise provided by the act, the Personal Data Act and appurtenant regulations apply as supplementary provisions, cf. section 2, third paragraph. Clinical testing of medicinal products on human beings is covered by section 3 of the Medicines Act and appurtenant regulations, which implement Regulation 536/2014/EU on Clinical Trials. The Medical Equipment Act and appurtenant regulations cover clinical testing of medical equipment. In this context, the provisions of this act apply as a supplement, where relevant.

350. Chapter 2 contains requirements concerning organization and execution of medical and health research. Medical and health research must be 'organized and carried out in a responsible manner', cf. section 5, first paragraph. Research must be based on 'respect for the research participants' human rights and dignity', cf. section 5, second paragraph. Furthermore, the 'participants' welfare and integrity shall have priority over scientific and social interests'. Medical and health research must take into account 'ethical, medical, health, scientific and privacy factors', cf. section 5, third paragraph. According to section 6, medical and health research 'must be organized as a project under the direction of a person or body responsible for the research' and managed by a project manager and must be described in a research protocol. The sources of funding 'must be' indicated in the protocol. The project must be subject to internal control 'carried out in a manner that is adapted to the size, nature, activities and risk factors of the research', cf. section 6 (*see also infra* regarding section 22).

351. The research project must be approved in advance by the regional committee for medical and health research ethics. According to the Ethics and Integrity in Research Act, the committee shall consist of members with skills in relevant discipline as well as in ethics and in law. Lay members shall also be included. Decisions regarding prior approval of the research project may be appealed to the National Committee for Medical and Health Research Ethics, cf. section 10, third paragraph.

352. The main rule on consent is stipulated in section 13, first paragraph. Consent must be obtained from participants in medical and health research, unless 'otherwise laid down in law'. Consent must be 'informed, voluntary, express and documented' and be based on specific information about a concrete research project (*see infra* regarding broad consent), cf. section 13, second paragraph. In order to ensure the voluntary element of the consent, section 13, third paragraph stipulates that if the research participant can be regarded as being in 'a relationship of dependency' with the person requesting consent, meaning that the research participant might feel pressured to give their consent, informed consent must be obtained by another person whom the research participant does not have this kind of relationship with. Consent to take part in a research project may be withdrawn at any time, cf. section 16, which also contain further regulation of the consequences of withdrawal (including destruction of samples, etc.). In the event of 'substantial changes to the research project', new consent must be obtained in accordance with section 13 if the changes are deemed to have consequences for the participant's consent, cf. section 15, first paragraph. If it is difficult to obtain new consent, the regional committee for medical and health research ethics may – if certain requirements are fulfilled – approve new or changed use of previously collected human biological material or personal health data without new consent being obtained, cf. section 15, second paragraph.

353. A legal invention in the act is the possibility of a broad consent, cf. section 14. Then the research participants may consent to 'human biological material and personal health data' being used for specific, broadly defined research purposes. A broad consent is practical in projects with a wide time frame, and where it is uncertain what exactly the researchers are looking for when the participants are enrolled. The regional committee for medical and health research ethics may specify conditions for use of broad consent and may order the project manager to obtain new consent if the committee deems it necessary, cf. section 14, second paragraph. Participants who have given broad consent 'are entitled to receive information' about the project at regular intervals. In practice this feedback is often given by websites for the project.

354. The regulation of competence to consent is to a broad extent based on the provisions in PRA section 4, but the rules are partly repeated and the text of the provision is rather technical. According to section 17, legally competent persons as well as minors aged 16 and over are competent to consent. For the latter group, otherwise may follow from statutory provisions or the nature of the activity. Such provisions are found in section 17 itself, third paragraph. Consent must be obtained from parents or other people with parental responsibility for research using minors aged 16–18 that entails 'bodily intervention or testing medicinal products'. The rules concerning consent stipulated in PRA section 4-4 apply correspondingly to consent to research including participants under the age of 16. If children between the ages of 12 and 16 do not want their parents, others with parental responsibility for them or the child welfare service to be informed about personal data relating to the child, for valid reasons, this wish must be respected. If the parents have joint parental responsibility, both of them must consent on behalf of the child.

355. The competence to give consent may cease to apply in the situations referred to in PRA section 4-3, second paragraph (if the patient is clearly incapable of understanding what the consent entails), cf. section 17, second paragraph. In such situations, the person's next of kin as defined in PRA section 1-3, litra b 'shall have authority to grant consent'. The relatives play therefore a more central role in medical research than in treatment (cf. *supra* 269). For persons been declared legally incapable of managing his or her own personal affairs pursuant to the Guardian Act, the PRA section 4-7 apply. The guardian can therefore consent on behalf of the patient.

356. Regarding research that includes minors and people who lack competence to give consent section 18 establishes conditions beyond the general rule in section 5. Research on these groups can only be carried out if:

(a) the potential risks or disadvantages for the person are 'insignificant';
(b) the individual involved is 'not averse to it'; and
(c) there is reason to assume that the results of the research may be of use to 'the person concerned' or 'other people with the same age-specific disorder, disease, injury or condition'.

For minors, it is a requirement that similar research cannot be done on people who are not minors, cf. section 18, second paragraph. For people who lack competence to give their consent, it is a requirement that there is 'no reason to believe that the person concerned would have been averse' to participating in the research project if they had the capacity to give their consent, and that similar research cannot be done on people who have the capacity to give consent, cf. section 18, third paragraph.

357. Prior to the Health Research Act research in clinical emergencies were normally impossible due to the consent requirements. In order to facilitate for research also in this situation, section 19 authorizes the possibility of research in emergency situation. If the patient is not capable of giving their consent and it is 'impossible to obtain consent from the person's next of kin', research may only take place if the following conditions are satisfied:

(a) the potential risks or disadvantages for the person are 'insignificant';
(b) the individual involved is 'not averse to it 'and there is no reason for researchers or other personnel to believe' that the person concerned would have been averse to participating in the research project if they had had the capacity to give their consent;
(c) it is 'only possible' to carry out the research in clinical emergency situations; and
(d) the research is 'justified beyond any doubt' on grounds of the prospect of results with major preventive, diagnostic or therapeutic value.

This provision is partly using the same conditions as research on minors and persons without the competence to consent, cf. section 18. If research is carried out in an emergency situation, the research participant or their next of kin must be given information about the research 'at the first opportunity', cf. section 19, second paragraph. Consent pursuant to section 13 is 'a prerequisite' for further research and must be 'obtained without delay'.

358. While the presented provisions are found in Chapters 1–4 and covering all forms of medical and health research, Chapters 5–7 regulates separate kinds of research. Chapter 5 regulates research involving humans. Such research may only be carried out if there are no alternative methods that are approximately equally effective. Before research is approved, 'the risk and hazards for the participants must be thoroughly evaluated', cf. section 22, first paragraph. The risk and hazards 'must be proportional to the expected advantages for the research participant personally' or 'for other people', cf. section 22, second paragraph.[151] Research 'must stop' if it is found that 'the risk is greater than the possible advantages' or 'if there are adequate grounds for positive, beneficial results' cf. section 22, third paragraph. Research 'may only be combined with treatment' if the research is assumed to have health-promoting value for the research participant, cf. section 22, fourth paragraph, which also provide guidelines for the assessment.

359. The project manager is obliged to report adverse medical incidents to the regulatory authorities about 'serious adverse and unexpected medical incidents' that are assumed to be linked to the research, cf. section 23. If research participants have been injured or if complications have arisen as a result of the research project, they shall be notified immediately, cf. section 24. Research participants are normally covered by the Norwegian System of Compensation to Patients (cf. *supra* Part I, Chapter 4, §1, I). The project manager is therefore obliged to inform the research participant about his/her right to seek compensation (either from the scheme or for other insurance schemes).

360. While biobanks for treatment purposes are regulated by the Biobank Act,[152] biobanks for research purposes is regulated by the Medical and Health Research Act Chapter 6, as well as research involving human biological material. Until the introduction of the Medical and Health Research Act, the Biobank Act covered all kinds of biobanks regardless of purpose. The provisions in Chapter 6 are rather detailed, and only some core elements will be highlighted here. According to section 28 the regional committee for medical and health research ethics may decide that human biological material collected by the health service in connection with diagnosis and treatment 'may or shall' be used for research purposes 'without the patient's consent being obtained'. This may only be applied if the research in question is of 'significant interest to society, and the participants' welfare and integrity are ensured' (cf. the similar wording in section 15). The regional committee for medical and health research ethics may specify conditions for use. The patient must have been informed in advance that in some cases human biological material may be used for research and must have been given the opportunity to refuse to be

151. *See* Sigmund Simonsen, *Acceptable Risk in Biomedical Research: European Perspectives* (Springer 2014).

152. *See* Marit Halvorsen, *Norsk biobankrett: rettslig regulering av humant biologisk materiale (Norwegian Biobank Law: Legal Regulation of Human Biological Material)* (Fagbokforlaget 2006).

involved in research on human biological material, cf. section 28, second paragraph. In order to facilitate the possibility of refusal, an electronic register is established with the details of the patients that have stated that they do not wish their biological material to be used for research.

361. According to section 31, the person or institution responsible for the research 'must grant other researchers access to human biological material in the enterprise's research biobanks', unless the person or institution responsible for the research needs the material or other 'exceptional grounds' exist. Guidelines for the assessment of 'exceptional grounds' are provided in section 31, second paragraph. Before material can be surrendered, the necessary approvals pursuant to Chapter 3 must have been obtained. Section 31 makes biobanks common goods for researchers. In addition to providing the society with the best possible research, the open access approach shall limit the strain on the patient with fewer requests from the researchers.

362. Research on medical data is regulated by Chapter 7. As with Chapter 6, the provisions in Chapter 7 are rather detailed, and only some core elements will be highlighted here. The processing of personal health data in medical and health research 'must have expressly indicated objectives', cf. section 32, first paragraph. The personal health data must be 'relevant and necessary' to achieve the objective of the research project. The degree of personal identification in the health data must not 'be greater than is necessary to serve the intended purposes'.

363. A revision of the use of medical data for statistics, analysis, quality improvement, research and similar purposes was made in 2020. The legal basis for such use was then formulated in one single provision in the Health Personnel Act, cf. section 29, instead of having parallel regulation both in the Health Research Act and the Health Personnel Act. The substantial provisions are still the same. Formerly, the competence was given to the regional committee for medical and health research ethics directly in the Health Research Act (former section 35), while it is now vested with the ministry which may delegate the decision competence to the regional committee for medical and health research ethics, cf. Health Personnel Act section 29, sixth paragraph. Use of medical data for research may only take place with a prior approval by the regional committee for medical and health research ethics, cf. section 29, fourth paragraph. The committee may decide that personal health data can be used for research. This may only be applied if the research in question is of significant interest to society and is unobtrusive out of ethical and medical considerations. The regional committee for medical and health research ethics may specify conditions for use. It should be noted that there are no exceptions for those opting out, like in section 28, second paragraph. The compulsory element was disputed during the legislative process of the Health Research Act.[153] The patients have no possibility to object for this distribution of health data, but it is accepted by the legislator as being a necessary tool for obtaining medical research. It should also be

153. Ot.prp. No. 74 (2006–2007) *Om lov om medisinsk og helsefaglig forskning (helseforskningsloven) (Regarding Act Relating to Medical and Health (The Health Research Act))*, 126.

kept in mind that Norway has many health registers of good quality, which enable epidemiological research when combining several registers with patient data.

364. Transparency and right of access to the research is regulated by Chapter 8, supervision by Chapter 9 and compensation, orders, penalties, etc., by Chapter 10. In total, the Medical and Health Research Act has become a rather detailed regulation. The aim of one mailbox is achieved, but the system is complicated and it could be difficult both for researchers and participants to foresee their legal situation.

§8. Euthanasia

365. As mentioned above, euthanasia is not allowed in Norway (*see supra* Part 1, Chapter 4, §1, II (Criminal liability), §4, II (Professional Codes) and Part 2, Chapter 2, §1 (the dying patient). The legal basis is the Penal Code section 277, second paragraph. Assistance to suicide is punished by eight to twenty-one years' imprisonment. If special circumstances apply, a shorter imprisonment or a milder kind of punishment can be imposed. If anyone out of mercy has taken the life of a dying person or who is at a terminal stage, a shorter imprisonment or a milder kind of punishment can be imposed, cf. section 278. In Rt. 2000 p. 646, a physician was given a suspended sentence for assisted suicide (*see supra* paragraph 168).

366. According to PRA section 4-9, second paragraph, a 'dying' patient is 'entitled' to object to life-prolonging treatment. The other flip of the coin is that health personnel are obliged to respect the patient's choice. The challenge is then to draw the line between the prohibited – and criminalized – assistance to suicide and the permitted objection to life-prolonging treatment. There has been some debate among scholar on this point. The core of the matter is the term 'dying patient', and the preparatory work provided limited guidance. Probably, it should be subject to a narrow interpretation. The body must be showing clear signs of being in a death process. Chronical patients where it can be anticipated that they will live for a while with medical treatment falls outside the scope of the provision.

367. The discussion of the matter will continue. Mass media stories of dying patients going to more liberal countries to end their lives fertilize the public debate. Additionally, there is an ongoing debate among the physicians (*see supra* paragraph 192).

§9. Others (Transsexual Interventions)

368. There are no statutory provisions directly targeting transsexual interventions. The national ID number contains eleven digits, where digit number nine indicates the gender (even number women and odd number for men). Those who want to change their gender must therefore apply to the National Register. The national ID number may be altered when gender status is changed, cf. regulation (14 July

2017 No. 1201) pursuant to the Census Act (2016) section 2-2, fifth paragraph. Either in the act or in the regulation further requirements is stipulated. According to long-lasting and firm practice, gender was changed when the Tax Administration – who is also responsible for the National Register – received a confirmation from the National treatment unit for transsexualism at Oslo University hospital. Such a confirmation was only issued to persons being diagnosed with transsexualism (ICD-10 F64.0), have undergone an extensive psychiatric assessment, including lengthy hormone treatment, and completed an irreversible sterilization (testicle or ovaries must be removed by surgery in order to change gender).

369. Several voices claimed that the Norwegian regulation and practice were too strict, and could also be a violation of human right obligations. The Norwegian Directorate of Health appointed an expert committee to review the current regulation and practice. The committee was composed of different professionals as well as representatives from the patient organizations. The committee found that the practice of requiring irreversible sterilization was not necessary for medical reasons and that many persons in the target group did not wanted to undergo this form of intervention. Furthermore, the committee questioned whether the strict requirements were in conformity with the human rights' obligations. The equality and Anti-discrimination Ombudsman held in a decision that contemporary practice violated the Anti-Discrimination Acts provisions regarding sexual orientation.[154] Due to this decision, the government appointed an inter-ministry working group to work parallel with the expert committee. Based on the assessments of the expert committee and the working group, the ministry submitted a proposition to the parliament.[155] The proposition contains an analysis of the current legal situation, including a comparison with selected countries and an assessment of the human rights' obligations. The Gender Change Act was introduced in 2016.

370. The Gender Change Act led to a fundamental change in the legal regulation of transsexual interventions. The process was simplified. A person experiencing or belonging to the opposite gender will is entitled to change sex based on application, cf. section 2. There is no requirement of diagnosis, expert assessment or medical treatment. If the person regrets the choice, he or she can change back to original gender. The act contains no additional requirements on 'second thoughts' and no limitation on the numbers of alterations.

371. Children over 16 years of age can on their own behalf apply for a gender change, cf. section 4, first paragraph. Children between 6 and 16 years of age must apply together with holder(s) of parental responsibility, cf. section 3, second paragraph. If the holders disagree, the gender should be changed if it is in the best interest of the child. The county governor in capital area (Oslo and Akershus) will then take the decision, with appeal to the national appeal body for health services, cf. section 5, second paragraph. Application from children less than 6 years of age must

154. 9 Sep. 2014, Case 14/840.

155. Prop. 74 (2015–2016) *Lov om endring av juridisk kjønn (Act relating to change of legal gender).*

be made by holder(s) of parental responsibility, cf. section 4, third paragraph. If the child is capable of forming their own views, the child shall be informed and given the possibility to express their view. It is a requirement for gender change of children less than 6 years of age that the child is born with an uncertain somatic gender development. The applicant must submit documentation from health personnel.

372. The expert committee suggested that person applying for gender change should receive an information sheet about the consequences, which in turn should lead to a confirmation of the application. This procedure was suggested in order to secure an informed consent from the person concerned and to avoid impulse applications. In the hearing paper, the ministry requests for feedback on this proposal.

373. When a person has changed their legal gender, the new gender shall as a main rule make the basis of all application of acts and regulations in other part of the legislation, cf. section 6. According to the ministry, this also applies in cases regarding affirmative action of the underrepresented gender.[156] However, some exceptions are stipulated in the act. The bodily gender shall make the basis if it is necessary to establish parenthood pursuant to the Children Act. A person changing his or her gender will keep rights and obligations pursuant to paternity, maternity or co-motherhood.

156. Prop. 74 (2015–2016) 31.

Part III. The Physician in Relation to the Healthcare System

Chapter 1. Collegial Relationships

§1. Associations

374. As mentioned above, the Norwegian Medical Association holds the position both as a professional association and as a trade union for Norwegian physicians (*supra* paragraph 239). Approved specialists are also registered in medical societies according to their specialization of the Association and are elected every second year by the representative body.

§2. Healthcare Centres

375. Many general practitioners, as well as specialists, are sharing facilities with colleagues, but there are a few provisions in the legislation regulating such joint activities. However, the requirement of responsible conduct in the HPA section 4 will apply on the individual physician. Additionally, facilities providing healthcare shall be organized in such a way that health personnel are able to comply with their statutory duties, cf. HPA section 16, first paragraph.

§3. Professional Duties Towards Colleagues

376. The professional duty towards colleagues is partly relating to the patients, and partly relating to a relationship between professional as colleagues. The first issue is to some extent regulated by different provisions, cf. the HPA section 4, second and third paragraph (*see supra* paragraph 135). Health personnel shall act in accordance with their professional qualifications, and 'assistance shall be obtained' and patients shall be referred on to others if this is 'necessary and possible', cf. HPA section 4, second paragraph. If 'the patient's needs so indicate', the profession shall be performed through cooperation and interaction with other qualified personnel.

377. In recent years 'individual plan' has become an important tool for patients requiring long-term, coordinated health services, cf. PRA section 2-5. Individual plans were introduced in health and social services, in order to coordinate health and care services, as well as other public services. Health personnel are obliged to participate in the work with individual plans, cf. the HPA section 4, second paragraph, last sentence.

378. Turning to the relationship between professionals as colleagues, there are few provisions in the legislation. This is considered more as a moral issue, which is partly regulated by the code of ethics for physicians (*see supra* paragraph 240). Part II contains rules governing the relations of doctors with their colleagues and collaborators. According to section 1, a physician 'must show respect for colleagues and collaborators, and assist, advise and guide them'. A physician who sees signs of professional or ethical laxity in a colleague or collaborator should 'first take the matter up directly with the person concerned', cf. section 2. The approach should be 'tactful', especially towards students or doctors in training. According to section 4, a physician 'should take care not to criticize colleagues and collaborators when speaking to patients and their relatives', but must always keep the patient's interests in view. Public and other debates between colleagues on medical questions and health policy issues must 'be conducted in an objective manner', cf. section 5. Physicians must communicate with one another 'openly and trustfully', cf. section 7.

Chapter 2. Relationship with Other Healthcare Providers

§1. PHARMACISTS

379. The two main legislative tools within the pharmacy field are the Medicines Act (1992) and the Pharmacy Act (2000). The Medicines Act regulates issues such as production, quality requirements, import, wholesale, retail and commercial of pharmaceutical products (cf. the definition of 'medicine' in section 2).[157] The Pharmacy Act regulates the activity of the pharmacies, i.e., licensing and requirements of the manager and the staff, sale and marketing and supervision. Pharmacists are regarded as health personnel according to HPA section 48, litra ø) and å) and the rights and obligations pursuant to HPA will therefore apply for them. Additionally, personnel in a pharmacy will be within the scope of the HPA if they provide healthcare, cf. the HPA section 3, third paragraph, cf. first paragraph, No. 2.

380. According to HPA section 11, only physician (and dentist) can make a requisition for medicinal products for which a prescription is required. Additionally, the ministry may by regulation give other groups of health personnel a limited entitlement of prescription (*see supra* paragraph 163). In 2003, the system of generic exchange was introduced, which also shifted the relationship between the pharmacists and the physician. The system was introduced to better enable access to market and to provide more affordable prices for the patients. According to the Pharmacy Act medicine shall be delivered precisely as prescribed in the requisition, cf. section 6-6, first paragraph. However, a pharmacy may exchange a prescribed medicine with a generic identical medicine or a parallel imported medicine if these have been approved as exchangeable by the ministry. Such exchange cannot take place if the patient objects thereto. The physician can also in the prescription indicate that generic exchange shall not take place. Such a restriction must be based on medical reasons, i.e., the patient is using several medicines and has difficulties with keeping them in order or is allergic or has experienced side effects with the additives.

§2. NURSES (MIDWIVES)

381. Nurses and midwives are health personnel according to HPA section 48 (respectively litra k) and v). Consequently, they are governed by the same regulation as physicians. As mentioned above, only a few provisions regulate the cooperation between different professionals. An overall guiding principle is the requirement of responsible conduct, cf. HPA section 4. This provision also contains a specific regulation of cooperation. The physician 'shall make decisions' in matters 'concerning medicine' in relation to examination or treatment of the individual

157. For a presentation of the supervision of the Norwegian Medicines Agency in English, *see* https://legemiddelverket.no/English (accessed 10 Jul. 2022).

patient. Even though not stipulated in law, nurses and midwives are obliged to follow the instructions given by the physician (with exception for instructions that are obvious wrongful).

382. Several decisions by the Norwegian Appeals Board for Health Personnel concern the lack of cooperation between physicians and midwives. A case where a midwife was given a warning pursuant to the HPA section 56 can illustrate some of the issues (25 January 2011, Case HPN-2010-210). After the amniotic fluid was miscoloured and the CTG was indicating limited heart activity, the midwife proceeded by her own, without calling for the physician. It could not exempt her from responsibility that the physicians at an earlier stage had approved the CTG. The midwife had an independent duty to carry out a continuous assessment of the condition of the foetus. If she was in doubt of the patient's condition, it would be responsible conduct to call for personnel with higher qualification, especially in cases where the outcome could be fatal. There were clear signs of insufficient communication between the midwife and the physician during birth, which the both were responsible for. The Norwegian Board of Health Supervision had not instigated proceedings against the physician, and the appeals board could therefore not make an assessment of his conduct. However, regardless of the physician's behaviour, the midwife's omission of calling for additional expertise was clearly irresponsible, cf. HPA section 4.

§3. Paramedical Professionals

383. The regional health enterprises are responsible for ambulance services, either by car, helicopter or boat, cf. the Specialized Health Care Act section 2-1a, No. 4. Many areas in Norway are scarcely populated, and the ambulance services are vital to transport patients to the hospitals. The regional health enterprises can either provide the ambulance services by themselves, or enter into an agreement with private or public entities. Like in many other countries, there has been a development in the equipment and personnel of the ambulance. They are partly working as a prolongation of the emergency unit of the hospitals, and physicians and nurses could also be working in the ambulances. Some ambulances are also specialized, for example, in taking care of psychiatric patients.

384. The responsibility of the paramedical professionals are – as nurses and midwives – considered as health personnel according to the HPA section 48 litra a). Consequently, they are governed by the same regulation as physicians. The provisions which regulate the cooperation between different professionals will be the same as mentioned above (*supra* §2).

Chapter 3. Relationship with Healthcare Institutions

§1. Hospitals

385. The regional health enterprises are responsible for providing hospitals, cf. the Specialized Health Care Act section 2-1a, No. 1. Most hospitals are publicly owned by the health enterprises, which in turn are owned by the regional health enterprises, cf. the Health Authorities and Health Trust Act section 2. Of the private hospitals, most of them will have an agreement with the public health enterprises and provide healthcare on behalf of the public. However, some hospitals are providing services directly to patients, outside the public system. All hospitals must be approved by the ministry prior to providing health services, cf. Specialized Health Care Act section 4-1. The provision also contains some guidelines for the ministry's assessment. It should be taken into consideration the public and medical need for the institution, if it is covered by the plan drawn up by the regional health enterprises and whether the services provided to the patients are of sufficient quality. An ongoing political discussion in Norway relates to the functions of smaller hospitals, *see supra* paragraph 3.

386. The hospitals are at the specialist level of health services. According to PRA section 2-4 second paragraph, the patient is entitled to choose between hospitals (and other kind of institutions) as long as the hospital is either owned by a regional health enterprise or is having an agreement with a regional health enterprise. However, the patient 'may not choose the level of treatment', cf. section 2-4, third paragraph. The patient is therefore dependent of the physician for referral to hospital or other forms of specialized health services. The general practitioner plays a crucial role in this loop of the healthcare system, by the monopoly of referral and this being a gatekeeper. The patient is entitled to a second opinion, cf. PRA section 2-3.

387. The previous Hospital Act contained a definition of a 'hospital'. This was not transferred to the Specialized Health Care Act, although it was not intended to change to content of the term, besides including psychiatric institutions.[158] According to the Specialized Health Care Act section 3-8, the hospitals have four dedicated tasks: (1) treatment of patients; (2) education of health personnel; (3) research; and (4) training of patients and their next of kin.

388. As in many other countries, there has, been an ongoing development in hospital services, where an increasing part of the services are provided at day-time without overnight stay. Another development is the distribution of responsibility between the primary and specialized level. From 1 January 2016, the municipality shall provide overnight stay to patients in need of emergency care, cf. the Health and Care Services Act section 3-5, third paragraph. Traditionally, the municipality has only been responsible for full time care, and not for emergency interventions.

---

158. Ot.prp. No. 10 (1998–1999) *Om lov om spesialisthelsetjenesten m m (Regarding Act Relating to the Specialized Health Services, etc.)*, 129.

The main aim is a better resource allocation, and increased cooperation between the specialized and primary level. In order to achieve better cooperation, the municipality and the regional health enterprises shall enter into agreements regulating the shared responsibility, cf. the Health and Care Services Act Chapter 6, which also stipulates requirements of the content of the agreement (section 6-2).

§2. Preventive Health Care

389. The main legal tool in preventive healthcare is the Public Health Act (2011), which was a part of the larger reform to strengthen the cooperation and division of responsibility between the primary and secondary level. The purpose of the act is 'to contribute to societal development that promotes public health and reduces social inequalities in health', cf. section 1. Public health work 'shall promote the population's health, well-being and good social and environmental conditions', and contribute 'to the prevention of mental and somatic illnesses, disorders or injuries'. The act applies to all levels of administration; the municipalities (Chapter 2), the counties (Chapter 4) and the central government (Chapter 5). Provisions regarding cooperation, emergency preparedness, internal control, supervision, etc., are found in Chapter 3. Additionally, the act contains rules concerning environmental health in Chapter 3. In such matters, the municipality is vested with different forms of restrictive measures, including rectification (section 14), coercive fines (section 15), suspension (section 16) and violation fines (section 17).

390. Provisions regarding preventive healthcare are also found elsewhere in the legislation. According to the Health and Care Services Act section 3-3 the municipality 'must promote health and seek to prevent injury and social problems' when providing health and social services. This should be done through, among other things, 'information, advice and guidance'.

391. The specialized level has similar duties pursuant to the Specialized Health Care Act, cf. section 2-1a, second paragraph. According to this provision, the regional health enterprises are obliged to, as a part of their responsibility for the specific services, to promote public health and prevent disease and injury.

392. The definition of 'healthcare' in HPA section 3, third paragraph also includes 'preventive' measures. Still, most of the provisions in the act regulate intervention of a current disease or injury, and the same pattern is found elsewhere in the legislation. However, the regulation concerning communicable diseases stands out as an area where the physicians also have duties stipulated in law concerning preventive measures. The aim of these obligations is to prevent the spreading of the disease. According to the Communicable Disease Act section 2-1, litra b), a patient infected with a communicable disease that is hazardous to public health shall receive 'individual infection control guidelines'. The obligation to inform can also include other than the patient, which could require an exception from the medical confidentiality in order to prevent the spreading of the disease. According to section 2-2 third paragraph, litra b), the physician can pass on necessary information to 'any person who in all probability is in a danger of being infected with a communicable disease that is hazardous to public health'. Several other of the provisions of the act have elements of preventive healthcare, some of them also of coercive character, cf. section 5-3 regarding detention in hospital (although rather seldom used).

§3. Health Insurance

393. Membership in the National Insurance Scheme is compulsory for all persons residing in Norway, cf. the National Insurance Act section 2-1. Others may be members on a compulsory basis, or based on application. However, membership is not based on health condition, although some benefits require that the applicant has been member for a certain time.

394. Private insurance – also regarding health – is regulated by the Insurance Contracts Act. In connection with the conclusion or renewal of an insurance contract, the insurer 'may ask for information about circumstances which may have significance for his assessment of the risk', cf. section 4-1. This obligation applies also when compiling information regarding health, but the act contains also some provisions directly regulating health information, or general provision which are of special interest of health information. The provisions in Chapter 13 were amended in order to regulate the insurance companies' collection, use and storage of medical information (27 June 2008 No. 65). According to section 13-1, the insurer can ask for information being relevant for the risk assessment. However, the insurer cannot ask for health information stemming from more than ten years behind, cf. section 13-1b. Furthermore, health information being collected or stored contrary to provisions stipulated by law cannot be invoked by the insurer. An example here is genetic testing, where it is prohibited – also for insurance companies – to ask whether such tests have been carried out, cf. the Biotechnology Act section 5-8, second paragraph (*see supra* paragraph 372).

395. HPA is – to some extent – governing the physician's communication to insurance companies. These provisions were taken into the act as a part of the amendment of the Insurance Contracts Act (27 June 2008 No. 65), and is incorporated in section 15 regarding requirements to medical reports, medical certification, etc. A medical report shall be 'correct, and contain only such information that is necessary for its intended purpose', cf. section 15, first paragraph. When health personnel understands that it could be of special importance how particular sensitive facts are described in a medical report to an insurance company, he or she should raise the issue with the patient, cf. section 15, second paragraph. When health information is shared with an insurance company, and the company understands that the information can indicate a serious disease, the patient should be informed first, if he or she is not familiar with the content, cf. section 15, third paragraph. These provisions were introduced to avoid a situation where the message of the disease was delivered to the patient by the insurance company.

396. In recent years there has been an increase in the private market and insurances covering health treatment. Of a population of 5.5 million around 648,000 has a private health insurance.[159] Such insurances will typically cover consultation by a specialist or a private hospital within fourteen working days and subsequent treatment within fourteen working days. Emergency healthcare is normally not covered. Most insurances covering health treatment are paid by the employer.

159. Figures from the end of 2016 provided by Finance Norway, https://www.finansnorge.no/statistikk/skadeforsikring/helseforsikring/, accessed 1 Jul. 2022.

Selected Bibliography

The following selected biography also includes works in Norwegian (with a translation of the title into English in brackets).

Anne Kjersti Befring & Bente Ohnstad. Helsepersonelloven: kommentarutgave (The Health Personnel Act: With Comments). Fagbokforlaget, Bergen 2019.

Anne Kjersti Befring, Helseretten (The Health Law). Cappelen Damm 2022.

Anne Hellum (ed.). *Birth Law.* Scandinavian University Press, Oslo 1993.

Asbjørn Kjønstad. Helserett – pasienter og helsearbeideres rettsstilling (Health Law – The Legal Protection of Patients and Health Personnel). 2d ed. Gyldendal, Oslo 2007.

Asbjørn Kjønstad & Aslak Syse. 'The Growth of Patients' Rights in Norway'. In *Patient's Rights: Informed Consent, Access and Equality.* Edited by Lotta Westerhäll & Charles Phillips. Nerenius and Santérus, Stockholm 1994, 255–278.

Asbjørn Kjønstad. 'Twelve Main Principles in Norwegian Health Law'. *Retfærd* 33, no. 3 (2010): 60–78.

Aslak Syse. Pasient- og brukerrettighetsloven med kommentarer (The Patient- and User Act – A Commentary). 4th ed. Gyldendal, Oslo 2015.

Aslak Syse, Morten Kjelland & Rolf Gunnar Jørstad (eds). Pasientskaderett: pasientskadeloven med kommentarer og utvalgte emner (Patients' Compensation Law: The Patients' Injury Act with Comments and Selected Issues). Gyldendal, Oslo 2011.

Elisabeth Rynning & Mette Hartlev (eds). Nordic Health Law in a European Context: Welfare State Perspectives on Patients' Rights and Biomedicine. Nijhoff, Leiden 2012.

Henriette Sinding Aasen, Rune Halvorsen & António Barbosa da Silva (eds). *Human Rights, Dignity and Autonomy in Health Care and Social Services: Nordic Perspectives.* Intersentia, Antwerp 2009.

Olav Molven (ed.). *The Norwegian Health Care System: Legal and Organizational Aspects.* University of Oslo, Centre for Medical Studies, Oslo 1999.

Olav Molven & Julia Ferkis (eds). Healthcare, Welfare and Law: Health Legislation as a Mirror of the Norwegian Welfare State. Gyldendal, Oslo 2011.

Selected Bibliography

Table of Cases

The numbers here refer to paragraph numbers.

Table of Cases

Index

The numbers here refer to paragraph numbers.

Index